Wearable & Decorative Stencilling

Patterns, Projects & Possibilities

Joanne Malone

Sterling Publishing Co., Inc.
New York

Photography by Victor France Photographics
Illustrations by Claire Daniels, Jenny Speechley, and Joanne Malone
Designed by Judy Morgan; edited by Isabel Stein

Library of Congress Cataloging-in-Publication Data

Malone, Joanne.
    Wearable & decorative stencilling : patterns, projects and possibilities /
Joanne Malone.
        p.   cm.
    Includes index.
    ISBN 0-8069-9446-0
    1. Textile printing.   2. Stencil work.   3. Textile painting.   I. Title.
TT852.6.M35   1997
746.6—dc20   96-38700
                                                                      CIP

1   3   5   7   9   10   8   6   4   2

Published by Sterling Publishing Company, Inc.
387 Park Avenue South, New York, N.Y. 10016
© 1997 by Joanne Malone
Distributed in Canada by Sterling Publishing
% Canadian Manda Group, One Atlantic Avenue, Suite 105
Toronto, Ontario, Canada M6K 3E7
Distributed in Great Britain and Europe by Cassell PLC
Wellington House, 125 Strand, London WC2R 0BB, England
Distributed in Australia by Capricorn Link (Australia) Pty Ltd.
P.O. Box 6651, Baulkham Hills, Business Centre, NSW 2153, Australia
Printed in China
All rights reserved

Sterling ISBN 0-8069-9446-0

To my family, Michael, Toby, and Georgia, and my mother, Dawn, brother Don, and all my other family members and friends for their immeasurable support throughout this and all of life's little challenges.

Acknowledgments

This project would not have been possible without the contributions of many people. I want to thank them for their parts in making this book possible:

❖ Michael and Toby Malone, for editing and proofreading

❖ Georgia Malone, for providing photographic assistance, quality control, and fashion advice

❖ Louise Allen of Piati Designs, for contributions above and beyond the call of duty in creating the clothes for the children's and fashion sections

❖ Models Lyndon Blue, Holly Verheggen, Elizabeth and Bramley Haran, Kelly Girdlestone, Kelly Gardiner, Louise Allen, and Bronwen Kahl

❖ Victor France, for his invaluable advice and expertise with the photographs

❖ Jenny Speechley and Claire Daniels, for the illustrations and patience

❖ Thanks also to Jan Janney and Robin Heenan of Crabtree Bay for helping with many of the projects in this book, and to Trish Rowe for creating the wonderful cape. Particular thanks to April Eddington for her home, which is featured in many of the photographs

❖ My heartfelt thanks also to my many friends, who contributed in so many ways, without whom this book could not have been completed—in particular, Gilly Furlong, Meredith Eddington, and Jan Bartlett.

Contents

4

Projects

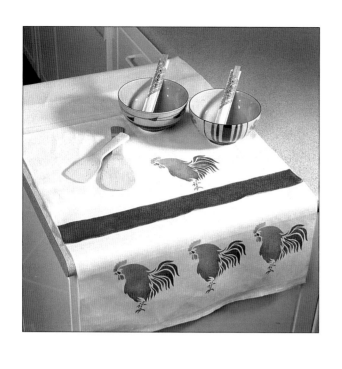

FASHION DESIGNS

CHILDREN'S DESIGNS

IDEAS SHOP

Introduction

Stencilling on fabric can open up a whole new world of creativity. Stencilling as a craft will open many doors to you. Exotic fabrics and ideas that you thought were only available in expensive stores can be yours if you open your mind to the opportunities around you. Create your own fabrics, your own designs, and your own environment. Develop themes around you in your clothes and in your home. Fabrics are wonderful to work with because they are so portable. Your house can remain very plain but have a maze of fabric accessories to dress it up and change it at will. This is especially true when designing for children; for example, you can match the quilt cover with the towels in the children's bathroom to take advantage of the latest crazes, so their surroundings can grow with them.

You can also choose to coordinate the designs on your walls, windows, and floors for a complete look. The amount you do and the simplicity or complexity of the look is your decision. It can have simple clear-cut fresh lines or an incredibly detailed and rich design that will give you many years of pleasure and make the hours of work well worth the effort.

This book concentrates on stencilling on fabric, but once you have mastered the techniques within these pages, you will be able to stencil on floors, walls, ceilings, and furniture, to name but a few other possibilities.

As well as being a book on how to stencil on fabric, this is a book of ideas—a book to inspire you to let loose your own creativity and discover all the skills you have. Everyone is creative in some way or another. Stencilling is just one way to express that creativity. Once you have started, you will find ideas everywhere.

Stencilling is addictive; once you realize how simple it is to achieve amazing results, it is very hard to stop. Husbands have been known to wake screaming in the night with visions of being stencilled while they sleep, only to find yet another swathe of stencilled fabric adorning their home or another bow stencilled on the wall. Don't laugh! Stencils even make a great temporary alternative to permanent tattoos for teenagers who are eager to decorate their bodies.

All the designs and ideas in the book are simple; you can make them more complex if you choose, but simple is a good place to start. The lines are clean and uncluttered, so they are easy to cut, and it is easy to appreciate the colors and work that have gone into the project.

It is a good idea to choose clear, bright colors, not only because they make you feel great, but because your family and friends will love them and they will continue to refresh your home and environment for a long time. However, you can also produce wonderful effects using soft, subtle colors to blend with antique furniture and finishes. We go into color in some detail in the color section, to give you more ideas.

We start with the basics, the "how to" of stencilling. If you are a beginner, read the Basics section carefully; if you have some experience with the craft, this section will refresh your skills so you can move onto the projects. We go through putting together a wall hanging step by step from the cutting out to the completion of the project. You don't have to actually do this project as your first one; you may want to start with one of the projects from the Simple Projects section instead. However, read through the Bird-of-Paradise project to get an idea of what is possible. There are many very simple things to make throughout the book as well, which are suitable to be your very first stencilled creation.

A fabric guide is included in the Basics part of the book—a wander through many of the different fabrics that can be used in the creative process, how they will react to the paint, some information about their construction and texture, and the best paints to use on each fabric.

Start stencilling with a project from the Simple Projects section—perhaps a tablecloth, throw pillow, or pillowcase—using cotton fabrics. You can go on to use one of the many ideas on how to design your home in the interior design section. Stencil curtains or upholstery fabrics to recover the family room chair. You can stencil your floor mats, rugs, or carpets, or make stencilled wall hangings or fabric-draped walls. The bathroom decor can be changed at a whim by stencilling the towels, bath mats, hand towels, or floor mats.

Children's clothes can also be individualized. Have a look at some of the gorgeous outfits in the stores and their amazing costs; then use the designs from this book to make something completely unique, using either ready-made clothes or those you have made yourself.

Speaking of clothes, don't you long to have something different, exotic without being over the top, stylish without being boring? Individualize store-bought clothes using ideas from the fashion design and ideas shop sections of the book. The possibilities are endless: from a whole outfit to a simple silk scarf; from a body-suit to a pair of jeans.

Where to start is often the hardest part. Designs, designs and more designs to choose from will get you started. They can be enlarged or reduced to suit your project. They can be simple or complex; it is up to you. Change them to suit your own style. Use this book as the basis for your creativity.

The inspiration for stencilling is all around you as you will discover: lace, leaves, china, drawings, books, flowers, and magazines are just some sources of ideas. You can stencil on anything that will stay still long enough, including all types of fabrics; it is just a matter of the right paint and preparation. Most important of all, have fun!

Some sources of inspiration for stencils.

THE
Basics

If you have never stencilled before in your life, this is the place to start. If you have done lots of stencilling before, this is the place to brush up on your technique and maybe learn something new. Stencilling is a very simple process. It is so simple that it is actually taught in kindergarten and primary school. It is basically the means by which a design is transferred onto a surface.

The art of stencilling is ancient. The fundamental process has not changed over the centuries, although it has been adapted to new paints and materials over the years. As a craft, it has endured where many others have died because it is not dependent on fashion or whims, but is rather a practical craft that adapts to the fashion. It requires no great artistic skill or ability, which gives everyone the opportunity to create items of wondrous beauty and simple elegance. If you are interested in the history of the art, there are plenty of good books available.

There are many different ways to stencil, materials you can use to make stencils, paints you can use, and ways that you can apply paint. This can all be rather confusing, especially when you are starting out. But don't despair, we'll review the basics here, so you can get started on what is really a simple and fun process.

Getting Started

Some basic stencilling tools, including foam paint rollers, sponges, stencilling brushes for applying paint, spray adhesive for adhering stencils temporarily, a cutting mat, drawing tools, a craft knife, masking tape, and paper towels.

Here are some basic supplies you will need for stencilling (1–9 below). A precut stencil is suggested for your first stencilling attempt so that you can focus on the act of stencilling, but you can cut your own if you prefer. We go into the process of stencil design and cutting in the next chapter (About Designs). When you cut your own stencils, you will also need items 10–13 listed below.

1. Acrylic paints, in colors of your choice*
2. Rollers, brushes or sponges*
3. Stencil
4. Something for a paint palette, e.g., a paper plate or old ceramic plate or tile
5. Roll of paper towels
6. Scrap paper for testing designs

*See individual projects for the colors of paints and the numbers of rollers needed.

7. Removable cellophane tape
8. Spray adhesive
9. Washable fabric marking pen or pencil or tailor's chalk for marking the position of stencils.

For planning and cutting stencils you will also need:

10. Drawing pencil, drawing pad, tracing paper, eraser, and drawing pen or fineline felt-tipped pen
11. Craft knife and sharp blades
12. Drafting film, sheet acetate, or some other stencil material
13. Self-healing cutting mat or several sheets of cardboard to protect your work surface.

THE WORK AREA

In addition to the supplies listed above, there are some basic things you will need for every project you do: an ironing board, an iron, spray starch, a ruler, and some pins. If you have a number of projects planned, it is a good idea to have a place where you can leave your work setup in place, if possible. A separate ironing board cover is also a good idea to protect the cover you use for your normal ironing from getting stained.

Iron, spray adhesive, and other things you will need.

WHERE TO FIND SUPPLIES

Setting up a network of suppliers where you can find all the bits and pieces that you need often can be one of the hardest parts of starting a new craft. There are three basic sources of the materials you are likely to need to stencil on fabric: craft stores, art or architecture supply stores, and hardware stores.

Craft stores will have most of what you need. An all-purpose craft store will stock paints of all kinds, stencil brushes, rollers, books, cutting mats and knives, as well as precut stencils. Most art and architecture supply stores will be able help you out with drawing pens, paints, books, cutting mats, and knives, as well as drafting film. Quite often, hardware stores will stock precut stencils, paints, and rollers. If you are considering attacking a large project like stencilling a whole bolt of fabric, the large rollers used for house painting will be easier to use than the small ones shown in the book. Bookstores often carry precut stencils, as well as a wide range of stencil books.

THE PAINTS

For stencilling on fabric, speak to your art supplier or craft store about all the different paints on the market. There are numerous types of paints for fabric, including plain fabric paints, paints that are mixed with a textile medium to make them work on fabrics, and all-purpose paints, which you can use on all surfaces.

Everyone has different preferences regarding the paints that they like to use—because of the color range, the texture, availability, the way the paints react to the fabric, or their ease of use. Ask friends, teachers, and the people who sell the paints for their opinions about what is the best to buy; this can prevent wasting a lot of money on something that doesn't suit your needs.

To practice on paper, ordinary acrylic paints are great to use if you already have some among your art supplies, but you don't have to rush out and buy some. If you are buying paints for a particular project, buy the ones you need for

Various kinds of paints for stencilling.

that project and use them to practice with first.

Always start any project by *practicing* on paper. I use butcher's paper or newsprint paper—clean white uncoated paper that comes in large sheets and is cheap and disposable. Old computer paper is excellent as well, but even the back of last month's school newsletter is fine to try out colors, designs and ideas. This is where you are allowed to make your mistakes.

Stencilling on fabric is really just the beginning. The techniques you learn for fabrics can be applied to walls, furniture, floors, or decorator items around the home to achieve a total look. You can stencil onto the furniture to match throw pillows, or stencil a dado (a border) on the wall to match the curtains, or on the floor to match the rug.

For stencilling on other surfaces besides fabric, the principles are the same. Use the right paints for the surface you are working on and practice on paper first. You can never use too much paper, and it is better to be sure than sorry. If you want to paint on walls or furniture, the best person to speak to about the right paint for the job is your local craft supplier or hardware store person. There are always new brands and types of paint on the market—the flavor of the month, so to speak—so find out exactly what will suit the project you have in mind.

When you finish stencilling, be sure the lids are screwed on tightly so that the paints do not dry out, and remember to clean around the outside of the containers.

THE STENCIL

You can create a stencil from just about anything. Many people use stencil cardboard (the traditional material that stencils were made from), a manila cardboard that has been treated with linseed oil to make it waterproof. This cardboard can be difficult to find, is hard, inflexible, and opaque, and is not the easiest material to use. You can also use old shirt cardboards, old X-ray film, or transparent acetate film (the kind used in photocopiers sometimes). Old wallpaper or plastic shelf covering (for lining kitchen cupboards) is also quite good.

Another option is stencil film, which is a fine opaque film that is wonderful to cut; however, it is very fragile and tears very easily. It is a shame to put so much work into something that will only last a short time. Be sure whatever material you use is not too thick—thick materials can affect the nice, sharp edge of the stencil design if you are not careful and are also more difficult to cut.

It depends really on how much you want to do and how long you want your stencil to last. Polyester film (Mylar®) is great if you want it to last forever, but it also can be very difficult to cut (and do your grandchildren really want to inherit your stencils?). I have found from experience that *drafting film* is easy to find, inexpensive, gives great flexibility for stencilling

around corners and curves, and is transparent; this makes it easy to transfer your design. Last but certainly not least, it is very easy to cut; a sharp blade will slide through the film without your needing to put much pressure on it at all.

Looking after your stencils: When you have finished painting, your stencil will have a slightly sticky backing from the spray adhesive used to adhere it to the fabric; if it is still very sticky, you have used too much adhesive. The top surface of the stencil will have paint on it, but it should not be wet; if it is, you have used too much paint.

The best way to clean the stencil is to lay it out on a flat surface on an old towel and gently scrub both surfaces to remove the paint and glue. If it doesn't come off, don't worry; just remove the worst of it. If you scrub too hard to get it all off, you may break the stencil, or it will wear out sooner than necessary. If the paint won't come off when you scrub it, it will definitely not come off on your next project.

Pat the stencils dry, and store them flat. Place paper between them: tissue paper, butcher's paper, or newsprint. If it is not possible to store them flat, you can roll them up with an elastic band around them. Before you roll them, place paper underneath each stencil and roll them together to prevent the stencil sticking to itself and to keep the finely cut parts from getting caught and torn.

If you have used too much spray adhesive, you may not be able to store stencils with paper between them as the glue will stick to the paper. Under these circumstances, you could use an old piece of fabric between the stencils, or use paper with a waxed or shiny surface.

Violet stencil with paint on it shows that all 3 colors were stencilled from one stencil.

ROLLERS AND BRUSHES

Foam rollers, available in paint stores, are a good way to apply paint for stencilling. Use one roller for each color, if possible. They come in several sizes, are easy to clean, and don't cost much. You will find that a lot of fabric paints (or paints with a textile medium added) can be very wet, unlike other acrylic paints. Be aware of this when you start using them, and be sure to remove all the excess paint and wetness from the roller or brush before applying it to the fabric. You know that you have taken enough paint off when the paint you roll onto the paper towel is no longer shiny and wet. You may find that the first time you use rollers, you will put far too much paint on your roller, until you get used to the technique. You learn quickly, though, as you realize how much paint you will waste!

The same basic rules apply if you are using a brush. Brushes are the traditional means of stencilling. Stencil brushes—short, round, stubby brushes—can be expensive. You can make your own, however, by buying inexpensive, 2-inch-wide (5 cm) housepainting brushes and cutting the bristles down so they are short and stubby. Many people believe you can achieve a better finish with brushes, but, like anything, practice makes perfect and it is very much an individual thing—what you get used to and what suits you. I personally find that it is easier and quicker to get a good finish with a roller; it also takes less practice! You will find as you do more and more stencilling that there are times when a brush works better—for a coir doormat or fabric with a thick texture, like towels, for example. Your choice of tools is purely a personal decision. Don't let anyone tell you one is right or wrong.

To load paint on a brush, dab it up and down in the paint, so the paint is just on the tip of the brush, then up and down on the paper towel to remove the excess wetness from the brush. As with the roller, any excess paint will ruin your stencil. "Bounce" the brush onto the surface of the fabric, through the stencil. You can create shadows and interesting effects by emphasizing different aspects of your design with more paint or different colors. Dab the paint onto the stencil, deepening the color as you go. Mask off your stencil, or cut separate stencils, if you prefer, for different colors. (See the section on cutting out stencils for details.)

Once you have finished painting, rinse out your rollers and brushes in cold water immediately if your paints are acrylics; the paint will come out quite easily. If you postpone cleaning up your tools until the paint has dried, you might as well throw them away. Some colors are more difficult to remove than others; you may need to rub the roller through some soap to

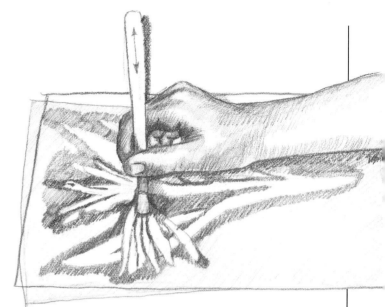

Bounce the paint through the stencil with your brush.

loosen the paint. Rinse your tools until the water runs clean and allow them to air dry; they dry quicker if you squeeze out most of the excess moisture first. If you are using paints that are not water soluble, use the appropriate cleaning agent.

Once they have dried, store your rollers with plenty of space around them in a dry plastic container or similar. Don't squash them too much or the rollers become misshapen and difficult to reuse. After washing brushes, stand them up in a container with the brush end up.

SPONGES

Interesting textures and finishes can be achieved using a sea sponge or even a kitchen sponge. For instance, if you are stencilling a brick wall, or anything else that is textured, a sponge can give a good effect. Cut the kitchen sponge into manageable-size pieces, about in quarters, and wet thoroughly. Squeeze out ALL the water in the sponge; any water left in the sponge will make the paint too wet, but is necessary to soften the sponge initially. Dab the sponge in the paint, take off the excess on the paper towel, and dab the sponge onto the stencil. If you want a textured look, do not overwork the area. The less you dab, the more you will achieve a texture. The more you dab, the more you will smooth it out.

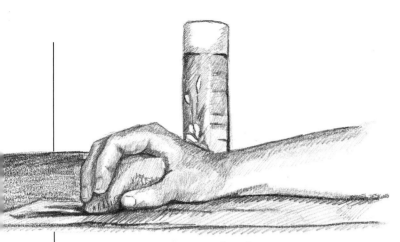

Using a sea sponge to apply paint.

SPRAYS

Spray paints can be very effective, but you have to be very careful with them. The paint is airborne, so you must be sure to wear protection for your skin and protection against breathing in the tiny droplets of paint. This means only use sprays outside or in a well-ventilated space, preferably one with an exhaust fan. Wear protective clothing, gloves, and a good face mask—one with replaceable filters, not the little paper masks, which are not adequate when you are dealing with paint fumes. It is necessary to mask the surrounding area of your work very carefully when you spray, because the overspray carries much further than you think it will. If you don't want to use an aerosol spray, it's possible to spray paint with a mouth diffuser. These are available in art supply stores.

Always adhere the stencil first with spray adhesive, as the spray paint will waft under the stencil and give a smudgy edge to the finished design otherwise. Don't use the spray adhesive when stencilling on paper, however, as the adhesive will stick the stencil to the paper permanently.

When spraying, keep a firm pressure on the nozzle of the spray can to avoid getting blobs of paint on the surface, and keep the can moving backwards and forwards across the surface to keep control of the amount of paint being applied. Apply a light film of paint and build up the color slowly, layer upon layer. If the spray is too heavy, the paint will run under the stencil.

Do not use enamel sprays on fabric for clothing or home use as they are not suitable. They are toxic and many contain lead. You can create some interesting effects if you use the enamel sprays on artists' canvas, but the sprays take a long time to dry and you must be very aware of the safety issues when you use them. Fast-drying acrylic sprays are the best to use on fabric, as the result is instant. Great effects can be achieved by overspraying with different colors.

Applying spray paint.

OTHER WAYS TO APPLY PAINT

All sorts of effects can be achieved by applying the paint with different materials. Experiment with a piece of paper towel scrunched up and dabbed in the paint, or cellophane, or cloth—virtually anything can be used, particularly if you are covering a large surface. Use your imagination, especially as you become more confident with the process.

A PRACTICE STENCILLING SESSION

By practicing on paper, you can play around with the colors, the depth of color, and the stencils to make sure you have them right. If it doesn't look right, try something else. Paper is expendable—your silk scarf isn't! You can cut out a paper replica of your project and stencil it to see what sort of effects you will get. Get used to it for a couple of days or for as long as you like before you take the plunge on fabric.

You may want to start out with a precut stencil. These are available at most craft stores, and at many bookstores and paint and design stores. While you are getting started, let someone else do the hard work of cutting the stencil, and just play with one for a while. You will find, after painting one design a number of times, that you want to try out your own design ideas and cut your own stencils, but using a precut stencil is is a good place to start. You will build up quite a library of designs to use and to mix and match.

tom. You may find you don't need the tape, especially with a small design, as you can hold it firmly in place with one hand.

3. Roll the roller in the paint, just enough to cover it evenly with a thin coat. Roll off the excess paint onto the paper towel, which will also have the effect of spreading the paint around the roller so that it will roll evenly onto the stencil. Too much paint on the roller will cause the paint to squidge under the stencil and give you fuzzy and messy edges.

Apply a dab of paint on your palette.

1. Place about a teaspoon of each color paint on the palette.

2. Lay the stencil onto the paper and hold it in place with the removable cellophane tape—a couple of pieces will be enough, top and bot-

Roll off the excess paint on a paper towel.

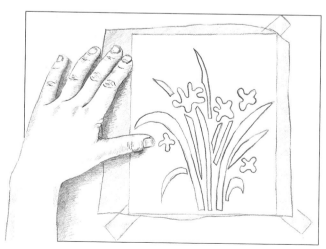

Tape the stencil over the fabric or whatever surface you want to decorate.

4. Carefully roll the roller back and forth over the stencil. Do not put pressure on the roller or it will push the paint under the stencil. You are really only taking the paint off the roller onto the surface being painted. This will give a very soft and subtle effect to your stencil. If you want a darker, deeper color, simply keep rolling the roller back and forth. You have complete control over the color. You can blend other colors in to give very sophisticated finishes, or you can have a very simple country look with solid colors.

Apply paint with a roller.

Regarding color mixing and stencils, you have a couple of options:

1. You can cut a separate stencil for each individual color. This takes a lot more time than cutting just one stencil.

2. You can cut only one stencil but cover the areas that you don't want to get a particular color by masking them with tape or paper. This also takes time.

3. As I have done with the Bird-of-Paradise, you can use one stencil and not mask it, but overlap the colors with the rollers, causing a blending of the colors. The bulk of the design will be the desired color, and the edges will have touches of the surrounding colors. This gives a lovely, soft look and movement to the design.

There are some instances where it is important that the colors be crisp and separated, but when you are doing an abstract design or a flower, the blended colors are much more appealing. If you look closely at a flower or leaf, you see it is never just green or just red or just pink, but a blend of colors, which gives the overall appearance of one color.

5. Repeat the process with each color for each part of your design. As you can see from the illustrations, only one stencil was used for the flowers and the leaves in this case.

6. Remove the stencil and enjoy your work of art.

Several colors were used on one stencil to create the Bird-of-Paradise flower. Two sheets of stencil film masked off most of the design when the deep purple was applied.

Lift the stencil and enjoy your handiwork.

HINTS

1. With store-bought articles, be very careful of the seams and hems. Either place the stencil carefully to avoid the seams, or place a piece of cardboard under the fabric to flatten the area. Painting over a seam can create a thickening of the paint; if it can't be avoided, apply the paint very lightly and carefully to avoid this thickening.

2. When stencilling an article that you are making yourself, apply the stencil before you stitch the article together.

3. Always heat-set the paint once it has dried completely, if the paint requires heat-setting. The paint should dry almost immediately after being applied. If the paint is still wet when you remove the stencil, you have used too much paint. You will find that some fabric paints will take a little longer to dry than others, so it is very important that you remove as much excess paint as possible from the roller or brush before you apply it to the stencil. The "little and often" principle is the best policy.

POSITIONING STENCILS

For a small project, you should be able to position your stencil by eye. For any project where the stencil repeats, its good to do some planning before you actually cut your stencils or do any stencilling. This way you don't waste any effort or have a disappointing experience. The plan for a large project (a sheet), taken from the violet sheet and pillowcase (pages 43–46), will give you some tips when you plan other projects.

1. For a rectangular project (e.g., piece of cloth, scarf, length of fabric, tablecloth), fold your cloth in quarters and mark the center horizontally and vertically by pressing, or with a fabric marking pencil. Measure the width of the cloth, subtracting any parts along the width that you don't want stencilled, and measure the width of each stencil (in this case, the bunch of flowers, the bow, the violet and leaves).

2. Make a small sketch of your project on paper (graph paper is helpful). Plan how many designs will fit across the width of your project. Remember to leave some room between designs in your planning. The designs could alternate, or the right and left halves of the project could be mirror images to name a few suggestions. If the designs don't fit well at the size you have them, enlarge or reduce your patterns as necessary on a photocopier to fit your plan. Then cut out your stencils. Note that you must size the stencils as you need them *before you cut out your stencils*.

3. If you want to stencil a border, you want it to align correctly all around. You can use registration marks, small squares or dots cut out that you use to align your stencil when you reposition it, to match up the pattern parts as they repeat, or you could draw a "repeat" pattern onto the stencil film, an extra design that you do not cut out, positioned correctly next to the one you do cut out of the film, so that when you reposition the stencil for the next stencil segment on the border, the uncut pattern will overlay the already painted design and the new segment to be stencilled will automatically fall into place. Be very careful that your paint is not wet when you use this method, as the wet paint will come off on the underside of the stencil and spoil your work. You can use tape to give you a nice, straight line to follow for your stencils.

Another way to stencil a large project, and perhaps the easiest in the long run, is to cut a piece of stencilling film the width of the fabric, transfer the repeat design onto the film, and then cut all the designs out. This way you only have one stencil to position and paint. You can measure the spaces on the stencil film and get the positioning just right. It takes a bit longer to cut out, but makes the painting a breeze!

4. For something with corners, create a corner stencil rather than trying to fit a long stencil into a corner. Calculate how much room you will have for corners, and use tracing paper to trace parts of the design, adapting it to the corner shape as needed. Remember to plan a well-designed link-up with the rest of the design. Then cut a separate stencil for the corner.

5. If you are stencilling a border onto a circular cloth, before you cut your stencil, fold the cloth in half, then in half again, and iron the folds to mark the four quadrants of the circle.

uncut (blocked-in) violet over a painted stencil, for registration

unpainted stencils

Position one stencil pattern over an already stencilled design so that the repeat pattern falls in the correct place.

18 Mark out your circle on the fabric in tailor's chalk or washable pencil. Decide where you want your stencils. Shape the pattern to fit the quadrants marked out on the cloth. Reduce or enlarge your stencil pattern as necessary; then cut out the stencil from drafting film. (See the Jonquil Tablecloth for adapting a circular pattern to use as a garland.)

6. For a stencil with more than one color, or one that is used more than once across something, you could include register marks in the 4 corners of your stencil. You can mark the position of the register marks when you do the first color by making a little dot through each register hole with a fabric marking pencil. When you reposition the stencil for the second or later colors, be sure the pencil marks show through the register holes and you will know your stencil is aligned correctly. I find it easier, though, to line up the design with the already-painted parts of the stencil.

7. Before you move your stencil for each repeat, complete all colors in that part. That is to say, position your stencil, paint the purple, then the green, then the white, etc. When that stencil is complete, remove the stencil and reposition it for the next repeat. It means that each section is finished as you go, which saves you having to go back over the design. Every time you try to reposition the stencil in the same place, there is a risk that it won't be quite right, and who needs that!

8. You can achieve a symmetrical effect by simply reversing the stencil. For instance, stencil the center bow on the sheet, cut a stencil with the violets and ribbons on it, and paint the violet stencil on one side of the bow; then reverse the violet stencil and paint it on the other side of the bow. Be sure the paint on the surface of the stencil is dry when you turn it over, so that it doesn't come off on the fabric.

If you make a mistake, don't panic. Mistakes often are wonderful opportunities to do something creative—an extra flower where you have a blob of paint, a swathe of ribbon to fill a space.

Symmetrical pattern in which right is mirror image of left.

FABRICS AND FABRIC PREPARATION

There is a huge array of fabrics on the market, which can be very confusing. The intention of this section is to give you an overview of the more common fabrics and how they will react to paint, the best way to clean them, and the best way to preserve the stencilled finish on them. This won't cover all of the fabrics available, but it is a starting point to give you a cross section of the reactions you can expect, so you won't have too many little surprises.

Natural fibers are traditionally the best to use for most craft projects. They absorb paint beautifully. There is nothing more satisfying than working with a soft silk habutai or a fine calico that has a lovely sheen and quality to it. However there are so many wonderful synthetics available to make a fabric artist's life easier that you would be mad not to use them. The color range is enormous, and many synthetic fabrics require no ironing.

Mixed fibers, which look like natural ones but have a small amount of synthetic mixed in, are great because you have the best of both worlds—the natural look with the advantages of synthetics (for example, less ironing). However, you will notice the difference in the way the paint reacts on the surface, even when there is a small percentage of synthetic in the fabric.

If in doubt with any fabric, paint a sample piece and set the paint as you would expect to; then clean it according to the manufacturer's instructions to see if the paint you have chosen will withstand the use that you have in mind.

Dupion Silk

This is beautiful fabric, finer than a raw silk or a silk shantung; it must be treated with care as it tends to fray with overhandling. You can use normal fabric paints or acrylic paints with textile additives to stencil any of these silks. Silk should be dry cleaned as many silks will distort, shrink, and lose their color if you wash them. It is a good idea to have a small piece painted and dry cleaned before you tackle any major project, because silk is expensive and you want to be sure that it is going to do what you want it to before you leap in with both feet.

To heat-set the paint, you will need to use a cotton cloth over the silk so you can make the iron hot enough to set the paint. Dupion silk was used in the wedding dress in the fashion designs section.

Silk Habutai

This is very fine, thin silk, which is usually used for silk painting or dying. It can be painted on quite successfully with normal fabric paints, but if you use special silk paints, it is necessary to use gutta, which forms little walls, to contain the paint and prevent it from spreading all over the silk.

You can stencil silk habutai quite normally, but because it is so fine, be careful not to use too much paint, because the fabric will become thick and hard. If you use a nearly dry roller to achieve a sparse look with the paint, the results can be wonderful. The paint can be heat-set with the iron, and the work can be either hand-washed or dry cleaned. Silk habutai was used for the silk scarves in the ideas shop section.

Velvet

Velvet can be stencilled quite successfully as long as you take into account the pile or nap of the fabric. If you run your hand over the surface of the material, the pile will either sit down flat and smooth, or become rough and untidy; the latter occurs if you rub it the wrong way. When you are stencilling, be sure to roll the roller along the fabric so that the pile sits flat; instead of rolling back and forth, only roll in the direction of the pile.

Dry cleaning is the best cleaning method for velvet. To heat-set the paint, simply iron it with a cotton cloth over the painted surface.

Coarsely Woven Cotton

This type of fabric needs more paint than others, and more pressure on the roller for the paint to penetrate the weave. Don't be tempted to put too much paint on the roller initially; in order to get a good coverage you will need to apply a few layers of paint. This is true of any heavily textured surface. To hold the stencil in place, use more spray adhesive than usual. This will not actually make the stencil sit flat on the surface, but will stop it from moving about. A bit more patience is required when dealing with this type of material. Coir mats fit into this category. The stencil will always sit a little above the surface, making it more difficult to achieve a clear-cut edge to a design. It is not appropriate to use spray paints on textured fabrics, because the paint will inevitably waft under the stencil, leaving an indistinct and messy edge.

Fabric paints can be used, because they soak well into fabric.

You can wash these woven fabrics; however, they will distort slightly, especially if washed in the washing machine. Hand washing or dry cleaning is preferable.

Iron the fabric to heat-set, using a cotton cloth over the surface so that the heat can get down into the texture of the weave. You could also use a hair dryer to heat-set, which may be easier, especially if you have stencilled on a large mat.

This is the fabric used in the woven mat in the simple projects section.

Satin

Satin may be made of natural fibers such as silk, or synthetic fibers such as nylon. The one shown here is a synthetic fabric, so when you apply the paint, it tends to sit on top of the surface rather than sinking into the fiber as it does with cotton or other natural fibers. Synthetic satin can be stencilled, but be sure not to use too much paint or it will build up on the surface and look quite thick. The synthetic fabric seems to repel the paint, which sits like oil on water. This is true of all synthetics so it is important before stencilling onto a fabric to know its composition. If you lay the normal amount of paint onto the stencil, you will end up with a ridge around the edges of the stencil, so work the paint very lightly and build up the color slowly. Heat-set the paint using a cotton pressing cloth with the iron set for cotton or on the hottest setting. Synthetics will not withstand the direct application of a hot iron necessary to set the paint; they will shrivel up, which is devastating after you have put in hard work to make a project. Synthetic satin can be hand-washed or dry cleaned. Silk satin should be dry cleaned. The three-piece suit in the fashion section is stencilled on satin. The "lace" evening dress is made of another synthetic, microfiber.

Synthetic and Cotton Sweatsuit Knits

This fabric is very easy to stencil. Even though it is a knitted fabric, it is fairly thick, so doesn't stretch very much when you are working on it. Sweatsuit knits are some of the most widely used fabrics, because they are inexpensive, comfortable, and wear so well. There are many different grades, from pure cottons, through different mixes of cotton and synthetic, to the pure synthetic. The rules about synthetics as explained in the satin section apply to sweatsuit fabric as well.

You can use any fabric paints to paint on sweatsuit fabric. How well the paint will be absorbed into the fabric depends on how much cotton is in the mix; the more cotton, the better the absorption. Sweatsuit knits are fully washable and so are great for children's clothes. Be sure to heat-set well, as this fabric will be washed often. If you need to heat-set a number of articles at once, they can be heat-set by placing them in the clothes dryer set to high for 10 minutes. The green frog sweatshirt in the children's section uses this fabric.

T-Shirt Knits

This material is perfect for stencilling. It may be all cotton or contain some synthetic fibers. You can use all kinds of paint on this material. Spray paints work quite well on T-shirts, as long as you have used spray adhesive to keep the stencil in place.

Check the content of the fabric; if it does have some synthetic, you will need to heat-set it using a cotton pressing cloth between the iron and the T-shirt, with the iron set to cotton or high, so the heat is high enough to set the paint but the fabric won't burn.

When you are stencilling a knitted fabric, be careful that it does not stretch and distort under the stencil. Rolling paint across a stencil can stretch the knitted fabric of the T-shirt, so do not press too hard when applying the paint. T-shirt fabric can be readily washed without losing its painted surface. The pansy, umbrella, heart, and sailing ship T-shirts use this fabric.

Cotton

Cotton is very easy to stencil; it is inexpensive and readily available, so it is a good fabric to choose to start your stencilling adventures. It is a natural fiber, so the paint is absorbed very easily. Cotton voiles are wonderful to work with, and are a much finer and more lightweight version of the cotton shown here. Cotton is the best material to use for curtains, tablecloths, quilt covers, and almost anything else you can think of. The only drawback cotton has is that it does need quite a lot of ironing, but then again you can't have everything!

Polyester–cotton blends are available with a 50/50 polyester to cotton ratio; they are great because they wash very well in the washing machine and need very little ironing. Cottons are easily heat-set with the iron set on high. The jonquil tablecloth and the voile curtains were made of cotton, as were the Christmas tablecloth and the fish shirt.

Denim

Denim is used in so much of our clothing. Not only jeans, but jackets, shorts, vests, and even upholstery can be made from this hardy fabric, which certainly has stood the test of time. It is great to stencil onto, because it is cotton. If you are working on denim that already is made up into a garment, you will need to think about where and how you are going to apply your stencil; pockets, studs, and thick seams need to be taken into account, but some fantastic results can be achieved with a little bit of imagination. A stencil dressed up with some embroidery or beading can look fabulous on denim.

All kinds of fabric paint can be used on denim, although spray paints can be a bit difficult if the garment is already made up. If you are creating the garment from scratch, there is no problem using the sprays. As usual, heat-set the paint with the iron on the high setting.

Washing the stencilled garment is not a problem; simply throw it into the washing machine, but don't scrub the painted area to clean it, or the paint may come off too. Avoid strong detergents, spray cleaners, and bleaches.

The denim vest with the sun stencil and the denim jeans with the spider stencil are examples of what can be done. The overalls with the engine design and the pink dress in the children's section are made of chambray, a very light type of denim.

Calico and Canvas

Calico is my favorite! It is the cheapest and easiest fabric to use. There are many different grades to choose from, starting with the refined seeded cotton that can be used for clothes or embroidery or fine craft work, and going through to heavier grades and unbleached calico, which can be used for curtains and upholstery linings and is characterized by a much coarser grain. Calico tends to have a lot of size (manufacturer's dressing) in the fabric; it is usually recommended you wash this out before using. This can be a very tedious task, especially since calico, being 100% cotton, takes a lot of ironing, which is no fun at all. If the article is not going to be washed when it is completed, don't bother washing it before painting it. If, however, it is an article of clothing or something that will require washing once completed, then it should be washed. It is wise to deal with the shrinkage before you cut the fabric out or paint it.

All fabric paints, including sprays, can be used on calico. Because it is cotton, there is no problem at all with heat-setting the paint or with washing.

Some of the projects in this book using calico are the Italian tablecloth and the poppy dress.

Canvas is another natural fabric, made of cotton, linen, or hemp. There are different grades and weights of canvas, from the finer canvas used for deck chairs all the way through to artist's canvas and tent canvas. All of these different grades can be treated in much the same way as calico when it comes to paint. However, test for shrinkage if you are making something that requires washing; some canvas shrinks quite a bit in washing. The teapot design place mats are made of canvas.

Homespun

Homespun is a loosely woven kind of cotton fabric with a somewhat coarse surface. It is very widely used in quilting, because it is available in such a wonderful range of colors. It should be handled in the same way as both calico and woven cotton. If the color of the fabric is intense, you will have to use a layer of white paint under your colored paint to keep the color of the fabric from showing through, or else build up your paint color in several layers. Homespun is good to use for tablecloths, quilt covers, quilts, throw pillows, and children's clothes.

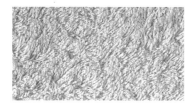

Towelling

Towelling has a wonderful texture, but this makes it a little difficult to stencil. However, it is cotton and so it absorbs paint beautifully. It is necessary, because of the texture, to apply more paint than usual; but don't use too much paint, or it will become thick and scratchy, which is not a good thing for a bath or beach towel to be.

Most towels have a texture or pile similar to velvet, but it is much less controllable. It is not enough to simply roll the roller in one direction on towelling. In order to get the paint in under the pile, it is necessary to roll the paint well into the texture of the towel. Practice on an old towel to learn how much paint is too much. There needs to be enough paint to give you a good depth of color, but not enough to end up feeling hard and crisp.

Heat-set the paint with an iron, or in the clothes dryer for ten minutes if you have a number of articles to do at once. You can see an example of stencilled bathroom towels in the simple projects section of the book.

Wool

Pure wool comes in many forms and is wonderful to work with, because it is a natural fiber. The wool fabric shown here is quite a heavy wool flannel and so is quite textured. You will find wool in knits, wool gaberdine, and lightweight wool fabrics, to just to name a few. Each of these has a different texture, but all will take the paint beautifully.

When painting wool flannel, consider the thickness of the fabric. It may take a couple of layers to work the paint into the surface; take care that the paint does not become blobby on the surface, particularly if there is any synthetic mixed with the wool. Woollen shawls, overcoats, and superfine wool T-shirts and leggings look wonderful stencilled, because it is not something that people expect.

The paint can be heat-set using a cotton pressing cloth over the stencilled area; the projects should be dry cleaned. Projects using wool in this book are the wool cape and the navy blue suit.

Linen

Linen, like cotton, is wonderful to work with. It has a more open weave than cotton, but not so much that it creates a texture on the surface. Linens are used mostly in items like dish towels or table wear (for example, Irish linen), not to mention heavy rich linens such as church linen. It is also used often in dressmaking, particularly in suiting, although it is notorious for getting very crumpled and often needs a lot of ironing, which tends to discourage many people. A well-starched, beautifully pressed linen suit looks absolutely fabulous. Linen is very durable.

Linen is very easy to paint, and linen dish towels make a wonderful fete project, or something for the kids to paint for aunties and grandmothers for Christmas. Be sure to heat-set them well, because they will be washed often.

All fabric paints are suitable to use on linen and are absorbed into the fibers very well. Dish towels and table linens can be machine-washed, but it is preferable to dry clean linen clothes. There are a number of fabrics incorporating synthetics with linen, which does make them easier to care for; they have more spring in the fiber. Linen and cotton mixes are great too. The items using linen in this book are the the Rooster and Geometric dish towels.

About Designs

CREATING YOUR OWN STENCIL DESIGNS

To get started, it is probably easiest to run down to the local craft store and buy a precut stencil to learn the painting techniques. However, it won't take long before you want to do your own thing. You can only use the one design so many times before going mad! The stencils in this book offer you many designs to choose from for cutting out your own stencils. Eventually, however, you will want to create your own stencils from your own designs.

There is inspiration for stencil designs everywhere you look. Once you get started, you will be seeing stencil designs in everything from the garden from seeds to fruit, and in magazine advertisements, fabric designs, and children's books; or you can draw your own pictures and turn them into stencils. Many designs can be adapted to make stencils by following a few simple rules.

You will need: a #2B drawing pencil, a drawing pad, tracing paper, an eraser, and a drawing pen or fineline felt-tipped pen that is fast drying.

A lightbox or light table makes your life very easy if you have access to one. Art and quilt supply stores sell these. You can make your own by putting a light underneath a glass-top table. A large window with sun shining through it also can serve as a light box. Just tape your design to

Sketch of Bird-of-Paradise flower and the actual flower on which it was based.

be copied to the window and tape your stencil film over that; then trace the design with a pencil or felt-tipped pen.

Most stencil designs are quite simple, though you will find that you become more ambitious as you gain experience. Start out with something simple that will adapt easily and that doesn't have too many difficult parts to cut out. As you gain more confidence, you can create some incredibly intricate designs using stencils as your base. Your imagination is your only limitation.

The Bird-of-Paradise (*Strelitzia*) design

shown here probably is a bit more complex than the stencils you will start with; it is included here for inspiration, just to show you what you can achieve if you try.

1. If you are creating your design from scratch, make a drawing of the subject (in this case the *Strelitzia* flower or Bird-of-Paradise), which will be the basis of your design. Simplify the lines to make them clear and concise. Try not to make a loose, tonal sketch, as this will make the next stage more difficult.

2. The uncut parts of the stencil within a design are called bridges. They hold the stencil film together and separate one area of paint from another. The bridge areas will remain without pigment. They should actually enhance the design and accentuate the main parts.

Lay a piece of tracing paper over the original drawing and trace it, creating bridges between the different parts of the design as you work. What we are trying to achieve is to break the design into forms that can be cut out so that the whole design still looks like a *Strelitzia*. If there are too many bridges, the final drawing becomes very broken up and loses its form; if there are not enough bridges, the design has no definition and the stencil doesn't work.

3. At this stage you can reposition leaves or petals to give the right balance to the design. You can draw one flower and one leaf from your vase or garden, then trace them as many times as you need to to create a bunch of flowers and leaves. You can use some artistic license here and adapt your drawing to suit the project you have in mind. In my design, the leaves have been moved around to fit the fabric.

4. To complete the drawing, place another piece of tracing paper over the top of the traced drawing and redraw it carefully with a fine black drawing pen or fineline felt-tipped pen. This will give you the final drawing that will be the basis of your stencil. This process may sound a bit tedious, but it gives you a chance to change the design, and also becomes your permanent record of the final design, if you ever need to reproduce it again. Think about the size of the parts of your drawing. Be sure they are not too tiny and hard to cut. If they are, enlarge your design on a photocopier before cutting your stencil. Check out the size of your design in

The drawing is traced onto tracing paper, and bridges are left between the parts (left). Parts of the design may be moved or left out as you wish, when you do your final tracing onto drafting film (right) for the stencil.

25

Example of bridges that are not well placed, because they break up the rhythm of the design.

relation to the project you have planned, to be sure it will fit well.

5. The last phase of the drawing is to transfer it onto the acetate film or other material out of which you have chosen to cut your stencil. I have used drafting film, which is similar to tracing paper, but is made from acetate and is much stronger in withstanding the paint. While you could cut your stencil out of tracing paper if you really wanted to, you would only be able to use it once, whereas the acetate film will last as long as you need it.

26

Another stencil derived from the same drawing.

CUTTING STENCILS

Cutting can be quite therapeutic as it requires concentration; you can forget about all the worries of the day. You will need the following supplies:

❖ A self-healing cutting mat; you can use a sheet of linoleum, glass, cardboard, or a pile of newspapers instead, but they will blunt your knife and make your job much more difficult

❖ A craft knife with replaceable blades (plenty of them)

❖ Your design and drafting film or other stencil material to fit over the design you want to use (cut the film so it extends a few inches extra all around the actual design)

❖ Drawing pen (e.g., a fast-drying, fine-point, felt-tipped pen)

To cut out a stencil, follow these steps:

1. Trace the design onto the drafting film using a drawing pen. Be sure to draw from left to right if you are right-handed (or right to left if you are left-handed), or you will find that the ink from the pen will smudge on the film, leaving you with black hands and a very messy-looking stencil. Check with your art supplier for a fast-drying art pen that is perfect for the job. You can use a pencil, but be sure it is *very* sharp.

2. Once you have drawn the outlines, it sometimes helps to shade in the areas to be cut out of the stencil. This is called *blocking in*. The lines on the stencil can be very close to one another and it can become very confusing as to what gets cut away if you don't block in. Cross-hatching the parts you want to cut out with pen or pencil on your stencil before cutting can simplify the process for you.

3. Cut a piece of drafting film to a manageable size; be sure to leave a border of approximately 2 inches (5 cm) around your design on a large stencil, or 1 inch (2.5 cm) on a small stencil. This prevents an overflow of the paint onto the background when you use a roller.

4. Take the pattern you want to make a stencil of and tape it to your cutting mat with masking tape. Carefully mark register marks in each corner of the pattern. Center the drafting film over the pattern and tape it in place. Start cutting: The secret of cutting out a stencil is to keep it moving! Rotate the cutting board as necessary to easily get to all the parts of the stencil. Be sure that your blade is sharp and change it regularly to ensure a nice clean cut.

The stencil pattern areas that are to be cut away are darkened or hatched so it is obvious where to cut; this is called blocking in.

Start cutting from the center of your design, and cut out the tiny parts first. You will find that if you cut the larger parts of the design first, it is more difficult to cut the fine detail. Cutting from the center to the outside keeps the design together as you go.

5. Try to cut smoothly and consistently, taking the knife off the film as little as possible, particularly on curves and straight lines. The more often you take the knife out of the film, the more bumps and knicks in the curves you will end up with. If you do end up with an uneven edge, you can recut it, but it becomes difficult to do this when you have an intricate design.

Cutting a stencil on a self-healing cutting mat.

6. On curves and circles, keep the knife in the film, and turn the design as you pull the knife through: cut, turn, cut, turn, cut, turn. This will give you a nice, smooth curve.

7. On corners and peaks, cut right into the corner to make sure the cut piece comes away from the film. If it is not completely cut out, do not be tempted to pull the piece—you will tear the film and will have to go into damage control. (If it is going to happen, you can be sure it will happen on the last cut on an intricate design, when impatience will get the better of you.) To cut an inside peak, cut across the peak and form an "X" with the cuts to get a nice clean point.

8. If the worst happens, and you do cut through a bridge or a piece that you shouldn't cut, don't panic—it is not the end of the world. Using brown plastic packaging tape, stick small pieces of the tape over the area of the false cut on the front and on the back of the stencil; then recut the stencil in that area. You will find that the tape will last as long as the rest of the stencil. Don't be tempted to use ordinary masking tape, as it will shrivel up as soon as you put paint onto it.

The most important thing to remember when you are cutting is to RELAX. Allow the knife to do the hard work for you. If your blade is sharp enough, you will not need to apply much pres-

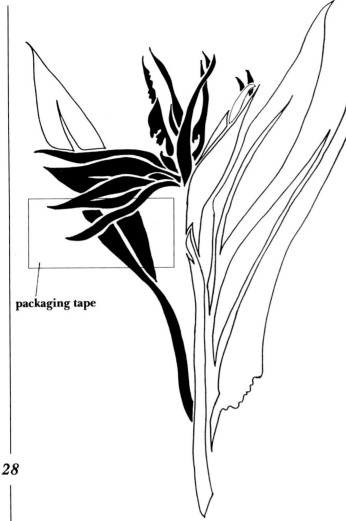

packaging tape

A stencil that is partially cut (black areas) may be repaired by having a piece of waterproof packaging tape pasted on both sides of the stencil over the false cut. Then it may be recut through the tape.

sure to the blade; simply guide it through the film. Position the film on the mat so you are always cutting towards yourself, as if you are writing. Allow the knife to roll in your fingers like a pencil. A round-handled knife, rather than a scalpel, is easier to use, although a scalpel

will do the job. Keep turning the film so you don't move, the film does. If you are starting to feel tense in your neck muscles, or your hand is becoming sore, look at the way you are cutting. Do you need to change the blade? On an intricate design, you may need to change the blade halfway through. It depends on the mat and the stencil material you are using, and how much cutting there is to do in the stencil. If in doubt, change the blade. The cost of the blade is small compared to the risk of spoiling your stencil. As the blade dulls, it will slip over the surface of the film instead of cutting where you want it to, and may make you tired and stressed. Relax, play some soothing music, and drift away; before you know it the job will be complete and you will be feeling wonderful. It is a bit like meditating. You don't have to think, just follow the lines.

ABOUT THE STENCILS IN THIS BOOK

All the designs have captions indicating whether they are the actual size or if they have been reduced or enlarged.

Any part of the design that has been drawn with a broken (dashed) line indicates that it should not be cut out; it is to allow for registration: matching up different parts of the designs.

These designs are a guide to get you started and to give you some ideas for your projects. The stencils can be mixed and matched, added to or subtracted from. The motifs can be used individually or put into a border, garland or whatever you choose.

Use the many resources around you to create your own designs, or adapt these to suit your own projects.

Color

There is a general belief that you are either "good" with color or you are not— an assumption that color is an instinct rather than something that is learned. This is not true. We can all learn about color. There are some very simple concepts to get you started; then it is up to you to play with your paints, and to experiment with stencils and color mixing to find out what *you* like and what suits your decor and taste. Each person has his or her own personal color harmonies that he or she is attracted to, and you will be happier for going on a voyage of discovery to find yours. You already work with color when you choose clothing, decorate a room in your house, or plan the arrangement of food on the table for a party. Mixing your own colors takes practice and some playing around, but it can be exciting discovering how easy it is to make your own palette of colors. You will begin to anticipate what you need to mix to achieve the colors you want. Hint: When you are playing with colors, write down how you created each color next to the swatch, so that when you refer back to it, you know exactly how to reproduce the same color.

What is covered here is very basic, and is meant to give you a taste of what is possible and an idea of how to get what you want. If you want to learn more, you can find books that go into more depth about color at libraries, art supply stores, and bookstores. If all else fails, you can always go to the store and buy a color premixed in the tube or the bottle. This costs more, but sometimes the time saved is worth it.

THE COLOR WHEEL

The color wheel, first invented by Isaac Newton, is a system for organizing and thinking about color. It is made by taking the visible spectrum of light (red, orange, yellow, green, blue, violet) and reproducing its colors in a circle. The color wheel helps you know what happens when you mix certain colors, and how to get the colors you need. We will talk about how to make colors from paint. If we were mixing light instead, our ways of getting colors would be different.

Primary colors: Theoretically, all colors can be created from three primary colors: red, yellow, and blue, darkened if necessary by black or lightened by white. There are actually a few colors, such as fuchsia (magenta) and bright orange, which you can't really mix from other pigments, but have to buy separately.

Pigments, the chemicals that color paint, are an attempt to get close to the pure colors (hues) of light. Pigments aren't perfect, and as you experiment, you will find that some reds are bluer than others and some are more orange, for example, which affects what you get when you use a particular red to mix colors. Speak to your paint suppliers and ask their advice as to which are the best colors to buy to form the basis of your color range.

Secondary colors. If you mix two primary colors, you get a secondary color: orange, green, or violet. Red + yellow = orange. Blue + yellow = green. Red + blue = violet.

Tertiary or intermediate colors. If you mix a secondary color with its neighboring primary color on the color wheel (for example, if you mix red and orange), you get an intermediate or tertiary color (in this case, red-orange).

Qualities of Color

There have been many schemes for organizing thinking about color. One popular one talks about three qualities of a color:

hue: what we usually call color; e.g., red, green, blue

value: the darkness or lightness of a color; for example, maroon is a dark value of red

chroma: intensity, strength, or brightness.

The color wheel, plus the concepts of hue, value, and chroma, help us learn about how colors behave.

THE COLOR WHEEL

Primary colors: red, yellow, blue

Secondary colors: orange, green, violet

Tertiary colors: yellow-orange, yellow-green, blue-green, blue-violet, red-violet, red-orange

The color wheel is a tool for studying colors and what happens when they are mixed. Complementary colors are across the diameter of the color wheel from each other.

30

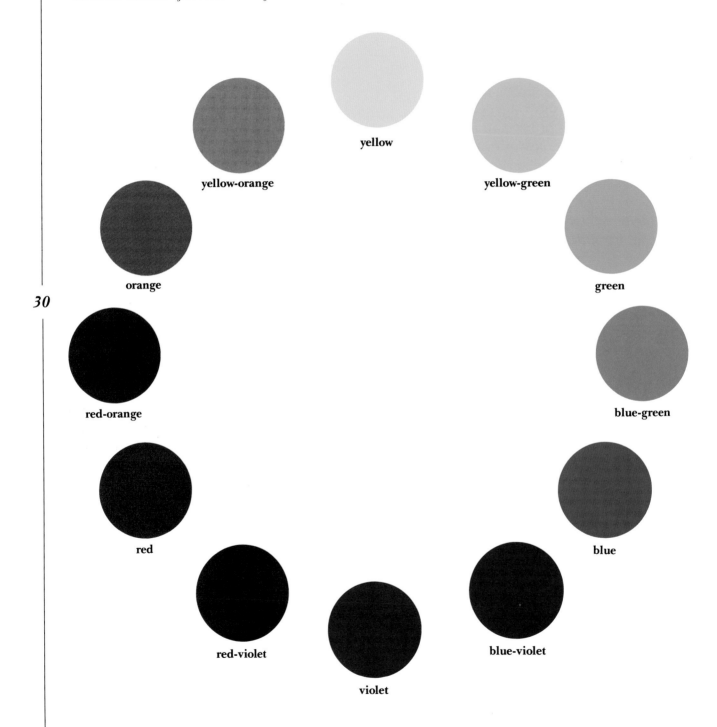

yellow

yellow-orange

yellow-green

orange

green

red-orange

blue-green

red

blue

red-violet

blue-violet

violet

Complementary Colors

If you take a hue on the color wheel and one that is directly opposite it on the other side of the wheel's diameter (e.g., red-violet and yellow-green), you have a pair of colors that are *complementary*. When you mix them, you get a neutral, grayish tone. You can lower the intensity of a color by mixing some of its complement with it. But if you put them next to each other, you get a very vibrant color reaction. A pair of complementary colors always includes one warm color and one cool color.

These two color "parents" can have many offspring. When you start experimenting with mixing them in varying proportions, and also lightening them by adding white or darkening them by adding black, you will start to discover the incredible range of colors you can create.

In the Bird-of-Paradise wall hanging, I used the complements of yellow-orange and blue-violet. You become familiar with complementary colors the more you work with them, and you will find that they can be very useful when building a picture. Using a complementary color can often mean the difference between success and failure. For instance, slipping some orange, apricot or terra cotta into an otherwise blue picture, or a dash of yellow in a mainly purple or violet picture will give the whole image a lift. (Apricot is a tint of orange and terra cotta is a shade of orange, but they are still orange.) When using complementary colors, be sure to get the right balance. You will find that too much yellow, in particular, can really overpower a design, but just enough gives the overall picture a real "zing" and highlights the design. Try placing a piece of emerald green fabric next to a piece of red fabric about the same size: the colors almost throb because they are complements, opposites on the color wheel. Next time you look at a quilt or a painting or a color scheme that is particularly pleasing to the eye, study the colors that have been used. Quite often complementary colors are used to produce that pleasing effect. They can be used in a very subtle way that you may not even notice at first glance.

Warm and Cool Colors

Colors have temperature. Red, red-orange, orange, yellow-orange, and yellow are warm colors. They remind us of fire or the sun. Warm colors make objects seem large and seem to come toward us. Greens, blues, and violets are cool colors, which remind us of lakes, the sky, or forests. Cool colors move into the distance and make objects seem smaller.

Analogous Color Harmony

As there are harmonies that you hear with sound, there are visual harmonies with color. The color wheel is a powerful tool in understanding these harmonies. The same way certain notes sound good together, certain colors look good together. We already talked about using a color and its complement together to create a complementary color harmony. Three colors that are next to each other on the color wheel (e.g., red, red-orange, orange) form an analogous color harmony, which is another good basis of organizing the colors in a project.

Monochromatic Color Scheme

At times you may find you want to make something that is based on only one hue, for example, blue, and its tints and shades. This is a monochromatic color scheme.

Tints and Shades

Adding white to a hue creates a tint. Adding black creates a shade. For example, pink is a tint of red, and maroon is a shade of red. Tints tend to look as though they move forward in a painting; shades tend to move away. When you add white or black to a hue, you change its value, which is another way of playing with a color and introducing contrast into a painting. Contrast is important in making a painting interesting.

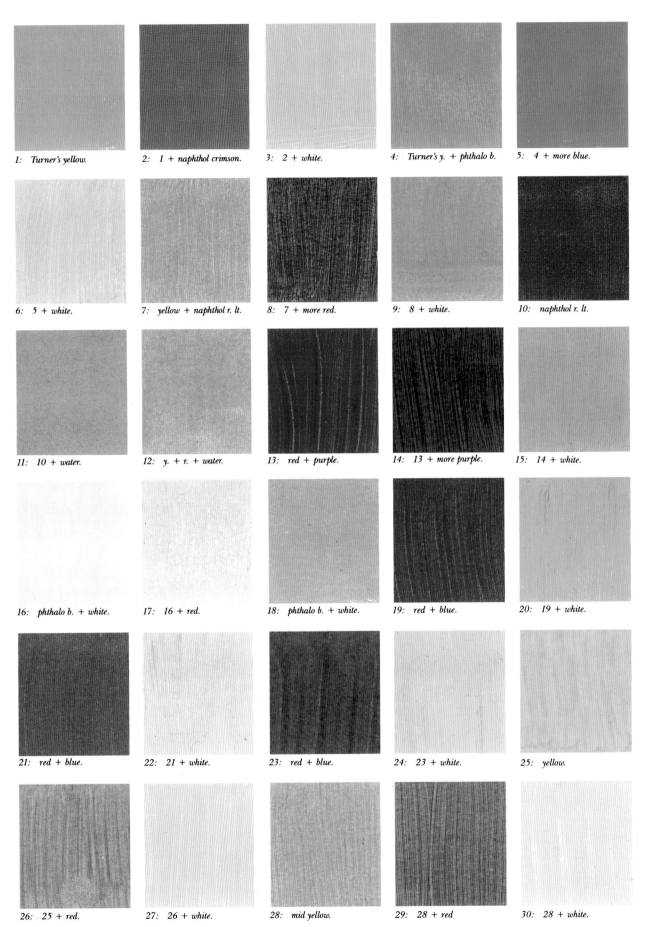

1: Turner's yellow.

2: 1 + naphthol crimson.

3: 2 + white.

4: Turner's y. + phthalo b.

5: 4 + more blue.

6: 5 + white.

7: yellow + naphthol r. lt.

8: 7 + more red.

9: 8 + white.

10: naphthol r. lt.

11: 10 + water.

12: y. + r. + water.

13: red + purple.

14: 13 + more purple.

15: 14 + white.

16: phthalo b. + white.

17: 16 + red.

18: phthalo b. + white.

19: red + blue.

20: 19 + white.

21: red + blue.

22: 21 + white.

23: red + blue.

24: 23 + white.

25: yellow.

26: 25 + red.

27: 26 + white.

28: mid yellow.

29: 28 + red

30: 28 + white.

Playing with color. Some color swatches derived from the colors of the Bird-of-Paradise flower. y = yellow; b = blue, r. lt. = red light.

A COLOR PROJECT: BIRD-OF-PARADISE WALL HANGING

The reason I chose this particular flower to illustrate my discussion of color is that it has so many wondrous colors in it. Have a look into any flower or leaf or shell, and you will see so many colors that blend and wash together to create the color that we see overall. A green leaf or red rose or a white shell is made up of many colors, which create the illusion of a single, simple color. Study a flower closely and recreate as many colors as you can by mixing your paints and painting a swatch of each color—you should be able to find at least ten! You will be amazed at the colors you will find, and will appreciate the complexity of nature in a whole new way.

You don't necessarily want to use all these colors in your final design (although you can create some very interesting and complex designs by using a number of them), but making them gives you some insight into how the final color you see is achieved, and will give your design depth and interest.

The stencilled Bird-of-Paradise flower.

Diagram showing how colors were applied to make Bird-of-Paradise flower.

I have chosen to use green, burgundy, purple, yellow, and lavender for my Bird-of-Paradise flower. The color was applied very lightly—the roller was virtually dry. It takes some practice to get this right; too little paint leaves your stencil dry and streaky-looking; too much makes it look thick with squidgy edges. Be patient and roll the paint on very lightly to produce a lovely soft, subtle color. Practice on paper or on a piece of fabric until you get it just the way you want it. The complexity of the colors gives it a luminesence which picks up the light.

Bird of Paradise wall hanging.

You can also stencil the fabric that goes on the back of your quilt, which not only reduces the cost but ensures that it is perfect for your project (quilt back pattern on page 133).

If you are not a quilter, you can still use the Bird-of-Paradise stencil (p. 37) to decorate linen hand towels for the bathroom, a pillowcase, a tablecloth, and many other things.

Fabric Preparation for the Project

Included earlier in this book is a guide to a range of different fabrics, designed to give you some idea of how they react to paint. In this project, I used cottons, mainly because they take the paint well, are easy to wash, come in good clear colors, and are easy to work with. You will need a fairly thin cotton fabric for the wall hanging front, such as calico or muslin, and an equally thin fabric for the backing and borders. You also will need washable polyester batting to go in between the quilt front and the back.

It is advisable to wash your fabrics before using them to remove the manufacturer's size and to preshrink the fabric, particularly if you are using 100% cotton fabric. If you are making an item that will not need to be washed, preshrinking is not so critical. Sometimes the size left in the fabric can make the application of the paint and ironing a little easier.

Once the fabric is washed, cut the quilt front into blocks (rectangles) and strips the size you need to fit your project. See the accompanying chart to know what sizes to cut to make the wall hanging shown. The sizes of fabric pieces given include seam allowances of ⅝ inch (1.5 cm) for each piece. Iron the blocks well to make sure all crinkles and creases are removed.

Enlarge your design to the size you want and cut out your stencil from stencil film or whatever you are using; cut register marks in your stencil also. Spray the back of the stencil with a light layer of spray adhesive. Lay the stencil on the center of the fabric piece to be stencilled.

Paint each color separately, as shown in the illustration on color (p. 33). Start with the green, then burgundy, purple, yellow, then lavender.

34

I used my stencilled blocks with the Bird-of-Paradise design to make a wall hanging, using traditional quilting techniques. The same techniques can be used to make a single, double, or queen-size quilt, or even a baby's blanket. If you choose your paints well, and follow the manufacturer's instructions, there is no reason why the wall hanging can't be used and washed regularly. The flower design is simple, so it can be easily reproduced, but you can substitute any quilting design you like for it. You can either stencil the blocks (the rectangles of fabric) or stencil the whole cloth of the uncut fabric and then cut it up and use it in your quilt. Stencilling creates endless opportunities for quilting, especially when you can't find that elusive piece of fabric to add that final touch to your project.

FABRIC PIECES FOR WALL HANGING

Code and Item	No.	Size (inches)	Size (cm)
A blocks	6	9.5 × 13	24 × 33
B short sashing	4	2.75 × 9	7 × 23
D long sashing	3	2.5 × 39.5	6.5 × 100.5
E top/bottom border	2	2.5 × 21.5	6.5 × 54.5
F side binding	2	2.25 × 42.5	5.5 × 108
G top/bottom binding	2	2.25 × 23.5	5.5 × 59.5
C backing fabric	1	26 × 48	66 × 122
batting	1	26 × 48	66 × 122

Masking for the Project

The colors in this design are quite separate, so it is necessary to mask off (temporarily cover over) areas where you don't want the colors to blend as you apply each subsequent color. There are a couple of ways to mask. You can cut one stencil for all parts of the design and use removable cellophane tape or an extra piece of paper or stencil film to cover up the cut parts which you want to remain unpainted for the color you are using. Or you can cut a separate stencil for each color. In this case, you only open up the parts of the design that will need to accept that particular color, and leave the rest of the design uncut. For example, if there is a red flower with green leaves, you would have one stencil in which the leaves are cut out and another in which the flower is cut out. You would stencil each color in turn, with its own stencil. Both would be aligned by the use of register marks. The method that I prefer to use, because it is quicker (I don't have to continually remove and reapply tape) and it works well, is to have a couple of extra pieces of drafting film handy to mask off the area that I don't want to paint. The film is easy to wipe off and reuse many times, and is very easy to reposition for each different color I want to stencil. You can use just about anything to mask—for example, a piece of cardboard or paper. You can cut and shape your mask to fit a particular project. You can even tape several masks together to create a little window for particularly difficult parts.

If you happen to get paint where you don't want it, use a cloth dipped in *cold* water and carefully rub the paint away. Don't use hot water; it will set the paint.

Heat-Setting

When you have finished stencilling all your colors, allow the paint to dry completely (which shouldn't take long if you haven't used too much paint), and iron the fabric on the wrong side, which will complete the drying process and set the paint on the fabric. Then turn the block right-side up; place a piece of cotton fabric, a large cotton handkerchief or something similar, over the painted area for a pressing cloth; and iron over it on the right side of the design. Using a pressing cloth is particularly important if you are painting on a fabric that contains synthetic fibers, because it will allow you to set the iron as hot as is necessary to heat-set the paint, without melting or damaging the synthetic. Iron the stencilled areas for about 2 minutes to ensure the paint is set. Some paints don't specifically recommend ironing to set the paint, but it is better to be sure than sorry.

(If you have a large project or a large number of items—for example, many T-shirts—to set, you can pop them in the clothes dryer for ten minutes on high to heat-set them.) Heat-set each block and the backing fabric if it has a stencilled design on it.

Completing the Project

Since the design and color were fairly complex, I was careful not to overpower them with the border of the wall hanging. I thought a textured fabric might be too fussy. Sometimes it is better to use solid colors in strips to highlight the design, or a small, overall pattern that isn't too noticeable. If in doubt, keep it simple. It is a pity to spoil all your hard work by using the wrong finishing touches. You can take your stencilled blocks with you to the fabric store and actually lay a few out on any potential border fabric, to see how they go together, before mak-

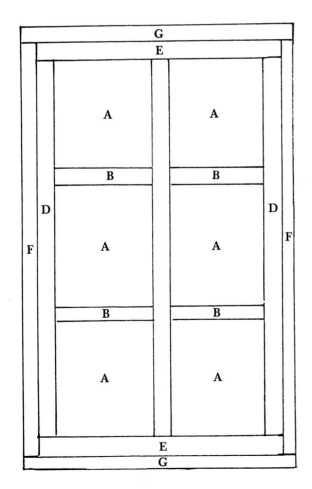

quilt
top

basting
lines

*Basting the three layers of the quilt
(dashed lines) to keep them from
moving while you quilt.*

backing

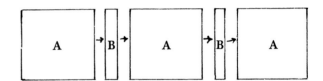

Making a row of three blocks.

*Diagram of the quilt top; see chart
on previous page for sizes of pieces.*

ing a purchase. Keep in mind the basics of color harmony when deciding on your border. You may pick up on one of the colors in your stencil and use a tint or shade of it, or of its complement. I used a shade of violet, one of the complementary colors in the flower for the border and sashing.

For the strips between the quilt blocks (short sashing strips, B), cut your chosen fabric in strips (see the chart for sizes) and stitch the blocks in two rows of three blocks each with the strips in between (see diagram). All stitching is done with right sides of fabric facing and seam allowances of ⅝ inch (1.5 cm). Then stitch a long sashing strip (D) between the rows of quilt blocks so that the quilt top is sewn together.

Cut two side borders (D) and stitch them on. Cut two of E (top and bottom border) and stitch them on.

When the quilt top is complete, iron all your seams flat so that they give a nice crisp edge, then cut your batting (quilt wadding) and backing fabric a few inches larger all around than the quilt top (see chart).
Center the quilt back, face down. Center the batting over the backing. Center the quilt top face up over the batting. Pin the layers together.

Carefully baste the three layers together (quilt top, batting, and quilt back) with a long running stitch, stitching from the center of the piece out to the edges; then quilt, either by hand or by machine. You can choose to simply quilt "in the ditch," where one fabric joins another, or you can highlight the design by quilting around the detail; my sample is hand-quilted in the ditch of each block. For a project that will be washed many times, it's better to machine-quilt.

Once the quilting is complete, you can bind the quilt. One way is to trim the batting and the backing fabric to the size of the quilt front (quilt top) plus seam allowance and bind the edge with bias binding.

Instead of bias binding, you can cut your own binding strips. Stitch on the side binding strips (F) and then the top and bottom binding strips (G) on the front, with right sides of fabric facing. Then turn the seam allowances of the binding over to the back and hand stitch them in place. Baste the edges of the three layers together before you attach the binding.

This project, which is more complex than many in the book, gives you some idea of the possibilities you can achieve with quilting.

38

Full-sized pattern for the Bird-of-Paradise stencil.

THE Projects

Simple Projects

Now that you have the basic stencilling technique sorted out, it is time to use it on some projects. The projects in this section are made on easy-to-stencil fabrics, like a basic cotton or calico. Consult the fabric guide section if you're in doubt about how a particular fabric will behave. If you are a beginner at stencilling, starting with simple items like dish towels, table napkins, and tablecloths gives you a chance to go over the stencilling techniques. Choose something that will lie flat without any bumps, seams, or folds, and fabrics that are not too expensive. If you choose to begin with something very complex, you risk failure, and we can all do without that. Always practice first. Have an old sheet or some bits of calico lying around to try out the designs and paints on before you venture onto the real thing.

You can follow the basic techniques of stencilling for most of the projects in the book, but I will give some hints along the way to help you solve some of the little problems you may encounter. The paint colors listed in each project show you how to achieve the look shown in the photographs, but they are only there as a guide. You will also need the basic stencilling tools and supplies listed on page 10. Use your own imagination and play with the colors to match with your own taste and decor.

Jonquil Tablecloth

YOU WILL NEED

❖ White cotton fabric or store-bought circular tablecloth

❖ Cotton sewing thread to match fabric

❖ Jonquil garland pattern

❖ Basic tools (see page 10)

❖ Fabric paints: warm yellow, white, light yellow (made by mixing white and yellow together), soft green

❖ 3 rollers or brushes

1. Measure the table for which you wish to make the cloth from the center of the table outwards to get the length you need, including the drop over the side of the table; add 2 inches (5 cm) for a hem. This is the radius (*r*) of the circle you need to cut.

2. Buy fabric that is at least as wide as the diameter of the circle (2 times the radius) plus a few inches. Fold the fabric in half edge to edge so that the folded width equals the radius of the circle you want to cut; fold the fabric down an equal length to the folded width, and mark a quarter-circle of the radius you need on the folded cloth (see figure) with fabric marking pencil or tailor's chalk. To get a fairly accurate circle, you can tie a piece of string of the radius you need to a piece of chalk and pin the other end of the string to the center of the circle; then swing an arc with chalk on the cloth.

3. Cut the circle out of the fabric. Put any excess fabric aside.

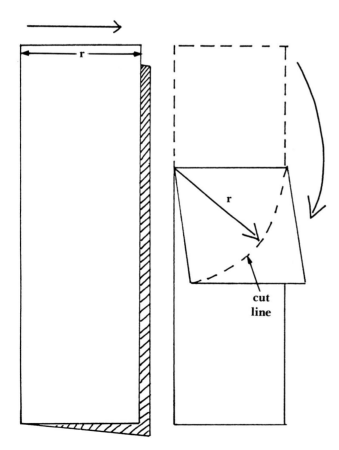

Fold the fabric in half (left). Then fold the top down for the length of the circle's radius (including hem allowance).

4. Iron the circle to remove all creases.

5. Enlarge the whole stencil pattern design from the book, trace it onto drafting film, block in the areas you want to cut out, and cut your stencil pattern from the film, including register marks. Plan out where you will position your stencils and mark their positions with fabric marking pencil. (See the basics section about cutting and positioning stencils if necessary.)

6. Spray adhesive onto the back of the garland stencil and place it in the center of the fabric circle.

7. Using your rollers, stencil the light yellow first, then the yellow in the centers of the flowers, overlapping the colors, and finally, the green.

8. For the border around the edge of the tablecloth, mask off part of the garland stencil as shown on the pattern, and repeat the stencil to create a swag border. Mark the register marks for each stencil on the tablecloth with tailor's chalk or fabric marking pencil, to be sure the garlands will line up when they meet across the bottom of the stencil, before you actually start using any paint. Then stencil the colors in the same order as for the central design.

9. When the paints are dry, use a pressing cloth and press the tablecloth on the back and then on the front to heat-set the paint (see general instructions); then make a quarter-inch (1.25 cm) hem. The best way to do this is to sew a long basting stitch around the edge of the cloth, about ½ inch (1 cm) in from the edge, gather the stitches slightly to ease the hem in, turn the hem under on the back, and fold the edge under again. Pin the hem in place and machine- or hand-stitch the hem.

10. With your extra cloth left over from cutting the circle, make matching napkins to go with the tablecloth in the same way.

41

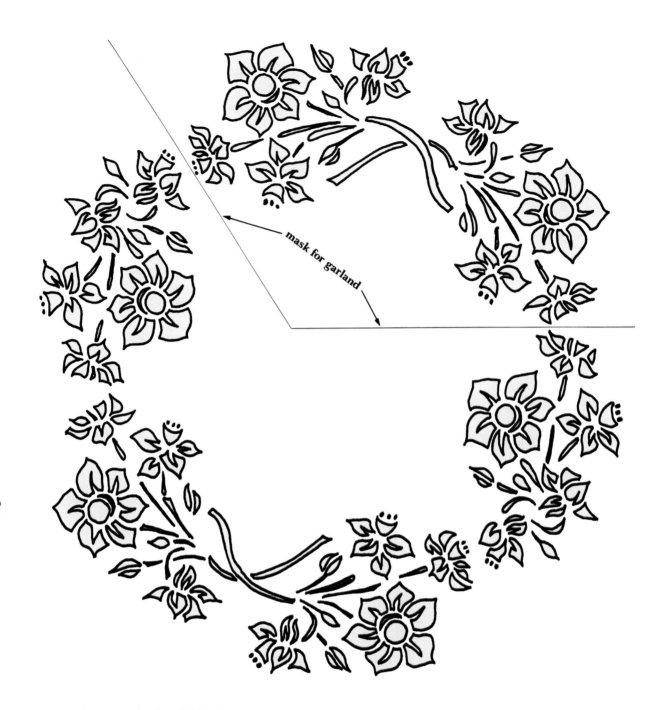

mask for garland

Jonquil tablecloth garland, at 50% of actual size. Photocopy at 200%. Mask off part to create the swag stencil for the border. Position the masked-off stencil as shown at right.

swag border

Violet Sheet and Pillowcase

YOU WILL NEED

❖ Solid color store-bought sheet and pillowcase

❖ Stencil patterns: violet garland, bow, and violet bunch (pages 44–46)

❖ Basic tools (see page 10)

❖ Paints: purple, white, green, black, gold

❖ Removable cellophane tape

❖ 4 rollers

❖ A few sheets of cardboard

Sheet

1. Read the section on positioning stencils in the Basics section before you cut your stencils. Adjust the stencil patterns' sizes if necessary and cut out your stencils from drafting film.

2. Iron the sheet to remove all the folding creases.

3. Fold it in half and mark center by gently creasing the fabric.

4. Place a line of removable cellophane tape along the lower edge of the sheet a few inches up from the edge, as a guideline for positioning the bottoms of the stencils. Repeat at the top edge of the sheet.

5. Place the bow stencil at the center of the tape line that runs across the sheet, and mark its position with a fabric marking pencil. Position the flower garlands to the left or right of the bow. (The stencil pattern has a reduced version of the garlands so you can see how they look lined up.) Working outwards from the center, mark the positions of your stencils to be sure they will be spaced well across the sheet before you begin to paint. Scatter the bouquet designs as you like on the main part of the sheet, marking their positions with fabric marking pencil.

6. Stencil your bows and ribbons in gold. Mix a shade of green you like with green and black. Stencil your flowers and garlands in the order purple, green, white. The white is at the center of the violets.

7. If you want the pattern for the violet and leaves to be reversed, make sure the paint left on the stencil is dry; then turn the stencil over to apply paint to the other side.

8. When the stencilled paint is dry, remove all the tape and heat-set the paint with the iron (see general instructions).

43

One stencil was used for all colors.

Pillowcase

1. To make the solid purple strip at the edge, measure and mark the distance in from the edge you want in tailor's chalk. Lay down a line of removable cellophane tape along your chalk line and another one a few inches away for the margins of your purple border. Load a roller with purple paint, and roll it along the border area; ensure even color by rolling back and forth.

2. Position the bouquet stencil in the center of the pillowcase.

3. Place a piece of cardboard between the layers of fabric just in case you use too much paint; this will prevent it seeping through to the back layer of fabric.

4. Stencil the bouquet: first use the green, then purple, gold, and white.

5. Remove the tape when the paint is dry. Then heat-set the paint with the iron (see basic instructions).

44

Bow, for violet sheet, actual size.

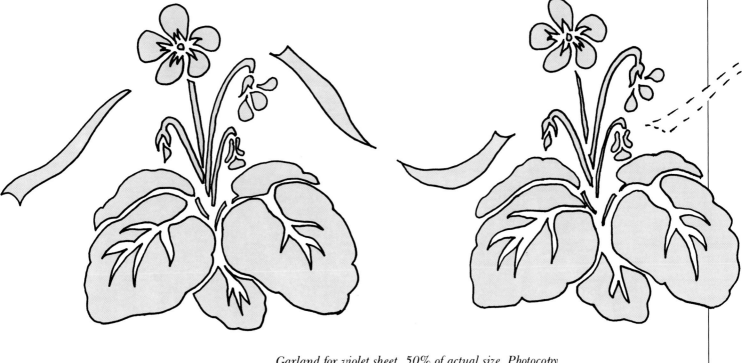

Garland for violet sheet, 50% of actual size. Photocopy at 200%. Dashed line is for positioning of repeat. Reduced garland below shows positioning.

Bouquet for violet pillowcase, actual size.

Rooster Dish Towels

Two dish towels; dish towel 1 (with three roosters) and dish towel 2 (with one rooster).

YOU WILL NEED

❖ 2 linen dish towels

❖ Paint: phthalo blue, yellow, magenta or red; green (mixed from yellow + blue)

❖ Removable cellophane tape

❖ Rooster pattern

❖ Basic tools (see page 10), including 4 rollers

Dish towel 1 has a border of three roosters; dish towel 2 has a single rooster, centered over a border. The blending of the colors gives the rooster an interesting effect.

Dish Towel 1

1. Put a line of cellophane tape across the width of the towel at the border as a guide to where you want your stencils to align. Mark the center of the line; that is where the center rooster will be positioned.

2. Enlarge or reduce the pattern size if necessary and plan the positioning of your stencils (refer to Positioning Stencils in the Basics section if necessary). Cut out the stencil from the drafting film. Using a fabric marking pencil, mark the position of the roosters.

3. Spray the back of the stencil with spray adhesive.

4. Mix a green from yellow plus blue. Stencil your colors, starting with green; then do the blue on the tail feathers and chest feathers.

5. Next do the yellow on the rooster's comb, jowls, beak and feet.

6. Stencil the magenta on the ends of the tail feathers, feet and the little bit around the beak.

Dish Towel 2

1. Apply a line of removable cellophane tape about 2 inches (5 cm) from the finished edge of the dish towel.

2. Mask off one rooster on the stencil and place one rooster in the center of the towel with its feet touching the top of the tape.

3. Stencil the paints for the rooster onto the towel in the same order as for towel 1.

4. To do the magenta border, place a paper towel or a sheet of scrap paper under the edge of the towel (see figure on page 48).

5. Load the roller with magenta, and roll it along the edge of the towel, so that it overlaps the tape edge and the dish towel edge. Ensure that the color is even by continuing to roll it back and forth on the fabric. Reload the roller with as much paint as is needed, being careful not to leave too much paint on the roller. There is a real temptation to put loads of paint on the roller, but you will end up with a sticky, wet mess on the fabric if you do; keep your paint dry and be patient.

6. When the paint is dry, remove the tape to reveal a nice crisp edge.

7. Heat-set the paints with an iron; see basic instructions section for details.

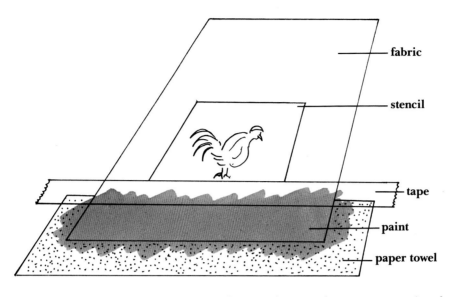

fabric

stencil

tape

paint

paper towel

Roll the paint for the border on the towel edge, overlapping the tape edge so you get a nice, sharp line when you remove the tape.

48

Roosters for dish towels, 63% actual size. Photocopy at 159%.

Woven Mat

YOU WILL NEED

- ❖ Woven mat
- ❖ Stencils
- ❖ 2 rollers or brushes
- ❖ Basic tools (see page 10)
- ❖ Paints: terra cotta (mixed from burnt sienna or orange and black), blue

1. Cut 2 stencils, one of each design.
2. Spray adhesive on the back on each stencil.
3. Lay the stencil in the plain area between the heavily textured stripes of the mat (this will vary with the mat you are able to purchase). Press down as firmly as possible onto the mat.
4. Load the roller and remove the excess paint. You will need to put more paint on the roller than usual, but start off conservatively. Paint the blue and the terra cotta, as shown in the photograph, masking the parts of the stencil as needed to prevent the colors from blending. When the surface is so textured, any subtlety in the color will be lost.
5. Heat-set with a hair dryer. (You can heat-set the paint with an iron, but you may find the hair dryer easier.)

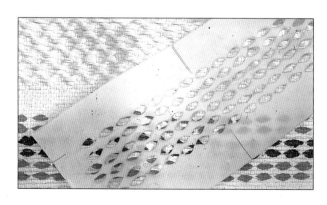

Above: first design for woven mat, actual size.
Left: closeup showing stencil.

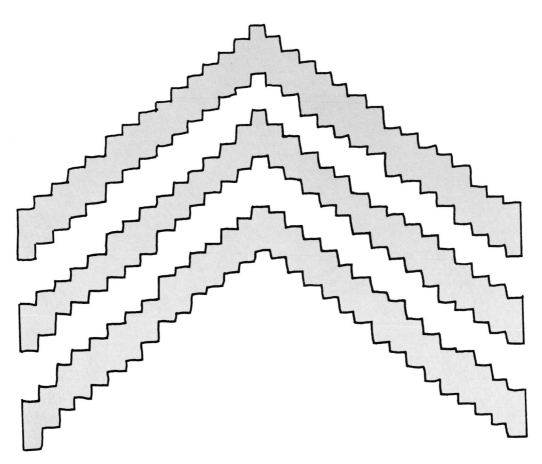

*Second design for woven mat, at 95%. Photocopy
at 105%.*

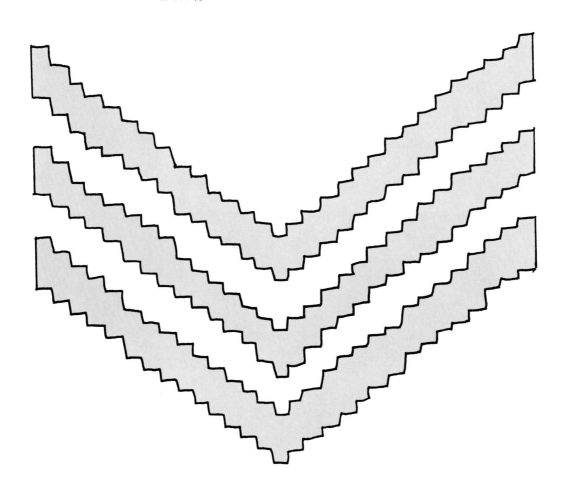

Celtic Throw Pillows

YOU WILL NEED

❖ 3 throw pillows or pillow forms

❖ Silk fabric (amount depends on the size of the throw pillows)

❖ Stencil patterns (pages 52, 53, and 54)

❖ Basic supplies (see page 10)

❖ Paints: olive green, gold

❖ 2 rollers

The instructions are the same for each throw pillow cover, but a different stencil is used for each one.

1. For each throw pillow, measure the size of the throw pillow front and add ⅝ inch (1.5 cm) seam allowance all around. Cut out pillow front. Cut the back about 4 inches (10 cm) wider than the top (the length stays the same), then cut it in two pieces to provide an overlap through which to insert the pillow form or throw pillow (see figure on page 52).

2. Enlarge or reduce your stencil pattern according to your pillow size. Cut out your stencil from drafting film.

3. Mark the center of the piece of fabric for the throw pillow top with fabric marking pencil or chalk. Spray the back of the stencil with a light spray of adhesive and center the stencil on the throw pillow top.

4. Carefully stencil your pattern onto the fabric, using the green paint, to achieve an all-over, even coverage.

5. Allow the green paint to dry; then roll a light layer of gold paint over the top of the green to highlight the design. The idea is for the gold to sit on top of the green, without having the colors blend together.

6. When the paint is completely dry, heat-set the paint by laying a pressing cloth of cotton fabric over the painted surface and setting the iron on cotton. Using a cotton pressing cloth allows you to use a high setting on the iron without scorching the silk.

7. Set the throw pillow top aside. Hem the edges of the two parts of the back of the pillow where they will overlap with a small hem, about ⅝ inch (1.5 cm).

8. Pin the back pieces to the front, with the right sides together, overlapping the back pieces at the center (see figure on page 52). Machine-stitch the back to the front with a ⅝-inch seam allowance.

9. Trim the seam allowances narrower at the corners to reduce bulk; then turn the throw pillow cover right-side out.

10. Press the seams flat and push the throw pillow or pillow form into its cover. You can hand-sew the overlap at the back closed if you wish, or leave it open so the throw pillow can be easily removed for dry cleaning the cover.

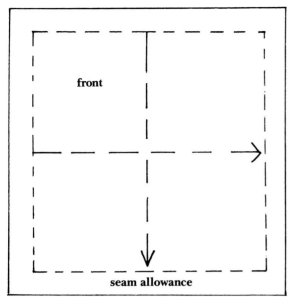

Measure across the pillow or pillow form; add a seam allowance.

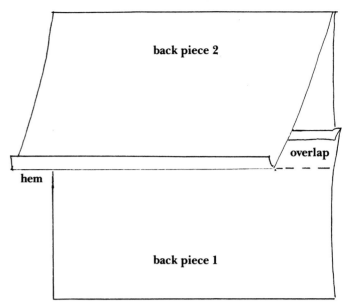

To make the back, overlap the back pieces at the center for an opening.

Celtic design for throw pillows (first of three designs), at 50% of actual size. Photocopy at 200%.

Celtic design for throw pillows (second of three designs), at 50% of actual size. Photocopy at 200%.

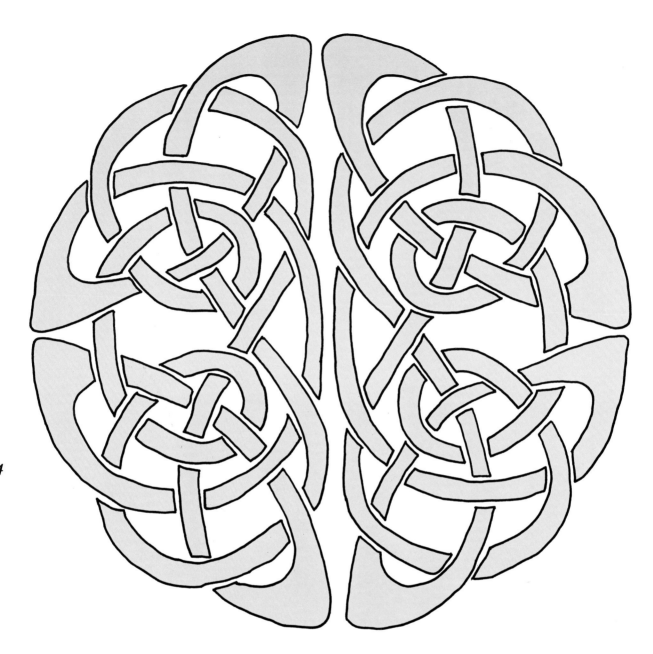

54

Celtic design for throw pillows (third of three 3 designs), at 50% of actual size. Photocopy at 200%.

Interior Designs

MAKING DECISIONS

Most of our interior design ideas tend to evolve over the years, reflecting changing fashion as well as a fluctuating bank balance: as we earn a bit more money, the prints make way for the original artwork. Not often do we have the opportunity to go through the whole house and change everything all at once; it would be nice to do, but it is often not very practical. When you move into a new place, it is time to make some major decisions: what to keep, what to get rid of, what can be revamped to fit in, and what will never make the grade.

How important is it to you to decorate in keeping with the historical period in which your house was built? While some people are overwhelmed by the beauty of a Victorian house, others may find the high ceilings and polished boards cold. Some may meticulously restore a 1950s house to its original glory, while many of us would see that as a waste of resources.

Most people like to have a feeling of continuity in their home, starting from the outside and going through all the rooms, to give a feeling of belonging and of making a house your home, even if you are renting.

You may choose to give an eclectic feeling to your home, using the best of different eras and a different color scheme in each room. That is entirely your choice. As with clothes, the fashion is what you choose to suit you.

CHOICES

What does all this have to do with stencilling? In a roundabout way I'm leading into the concept of choice—being able to choose what you want and reducing your limitations. Instead of being limited by cost, resources, and other people's ideas, when you stencil, your *only* limitation is your own imagination. If you think you don't

have one (and you do, you know), use someone else's. There are thousands of ideas published daily in magazines, books, newspapers— virtually anywhere you care to look. Your children come home with ideas, your friends have them—use all the resources available to you to extend and develop your ideas. The more you do, the more you stimulate your own ideas.

Stencilling is portable. You might be nervous about putting paint directly onto your walls or floors, but something that can be removed or changed if you don't like it or if you get tired of it offers many possibilities. The interior design section helps you to brainstorm some ideas. Some of them you may have heard of before, some you may never have considered doing, but now is your chance to give it a go, not necessarily to produce a stencilled look, but as an alternative to more conventional and more expensive options.

You can sew your own curtains or purchase ready-made ones, and stencil them to create an illusion. The ideas shown here are simple—you need no great skill to achieve them. They are a starting point, so please don't stop with these.

In the bathroom, by simply changing the towels, you can have a completely different theme every week. I know that sounds extreme, but think about it. If you paint your bathroom a relatively neutral color—white, cream, beige, or peach—you can change the look with your towels. Purchase good-quality towels (not necessarily the most expensive) or sets of towels, bathmats, and washcloths in several different colors. Stencil a different theme on each set to change the mood in the bathroom.

For instance, on the blue towels, use a nautical theme; on the apricot towels, what about sea shells? Choose a darker color towel and stencil it in a pale color for a dramatic look. Some spring flowers on white towels will make you feel wonderful in the midst of a cold winter (see the towels and washcloths project for examples of this).

If you want to really get into the swing of it, keep a conch shell or a collection of shells with matching guest soaps in the cupboard to bring out to match the towels, or a bunch of spring flowers in a vase to complement your flower stencil. It doesn't take much to create a theme. If you keep the basics simple and uncluttered, the addition of a plant or an ornament can change the whole room.

How about some elephants for an African theme? Perhaps you can find some elephant soaps, and stencilling some cute elephants on the towels to match will create a real conversation piece.

In addition to stencilling curtains, you can create a different look in the bedroom by stencilling a new quilt cover or quilt. Change it on a weekly basis, if you want to. This is especially wonderful in a child's room. Use designs based on whatever happens to be the most popular image for that week—cartoon characters, teddy bears, jungle animals, or rock music idols. The design could even be based on a drawing created by your child.

Stencilling on your floors can be a real treat. You can stencil the wooden floor or add stencilled rugs tossed about on your existing carpet or on a wooden floor. You can actually create a Persian-style rug with stencilling, if you are prepared to put in the time and effort to cut the intricate design.

Many kitchen items—including canvas mats, dish towels, hand towels, oven mitts, and aprons—can be stencilled to give a theme to your kitchen. You may be restricted by the existing colors, but if you start out with a neutral kitchen color, you can change the look as you please. You can even choose a color scheme to match your dishes.

❖❖❖❖❖❖❖❖❖❖❖❖

Voile Curtains with Rope Design

YOU WILL NEED

❖ 45-inch-wide (115 cm) white voile in lengths to reach the floor (approximately 3-yard (3 m) lengths. The number of lengths you need depends on the width of the window.

❖ Basic supplies (see page 10)

❖ Rope stencil pattern

❖ Paints: purple (or red and blue mixed to make purple), gold

1. Enlarge the pattern and cut out the stencil from drafting film (see general instructions).
2. Hem the ends of the lengths of fabric.
3. Iron the panels to remove all wrinkles.
4. Lay out the fabric. Put a line of removable tape along the bottom and sides of the panel where you want to stencil sections to align; this will guide you in positioning them. Stencil the rope design, starting from a corner. Reverse the stencil to do the opposite corner, to achieve a mirror image.
5. Stencil all the fabric pieces with purple, then gold over it. Be sure that the purple is dry before applying the gold. The gold is a highlight, so you don't want it to blend. Don't apply the gold paint too heavily or it will take over the purple.
6. Heat-set the paint with an iron (see basic instructions).
7. To achieve the draped effect, mount a curtain rod across the window (see photo). If it is a wide window, you will need a support in the middle of the window frame as well as at each end. Drape one length of fabric (Drape 1) from the end of the rod to the center of the window, and do the same for the panel at the the other end so that they may overlap (Drape 2).

Carefully drape another length (Drape 3) across the center. Simply tuck the ends of the third panel over the curtain rod; it should stay in place with the other drapes holding it firm. Take two pieces for each end of the curtain rod, gather them in, tuck the ends over the rod, and adjust the gathers. You may choose to have more lengths, depending on how full you want the curtains. In the photo, the width of the window appears wider because the curtains extend onto the wall area. The only disadvantage with this style of curtain is that you cannot draw the curtains for privacy, but you could hang a sheer curtain on a second rod behind the curtains. The window treatment does look great, however, and allows plenty of light into the room. Adjust the folds of the curtains so the stencils on the fabric are seen well.

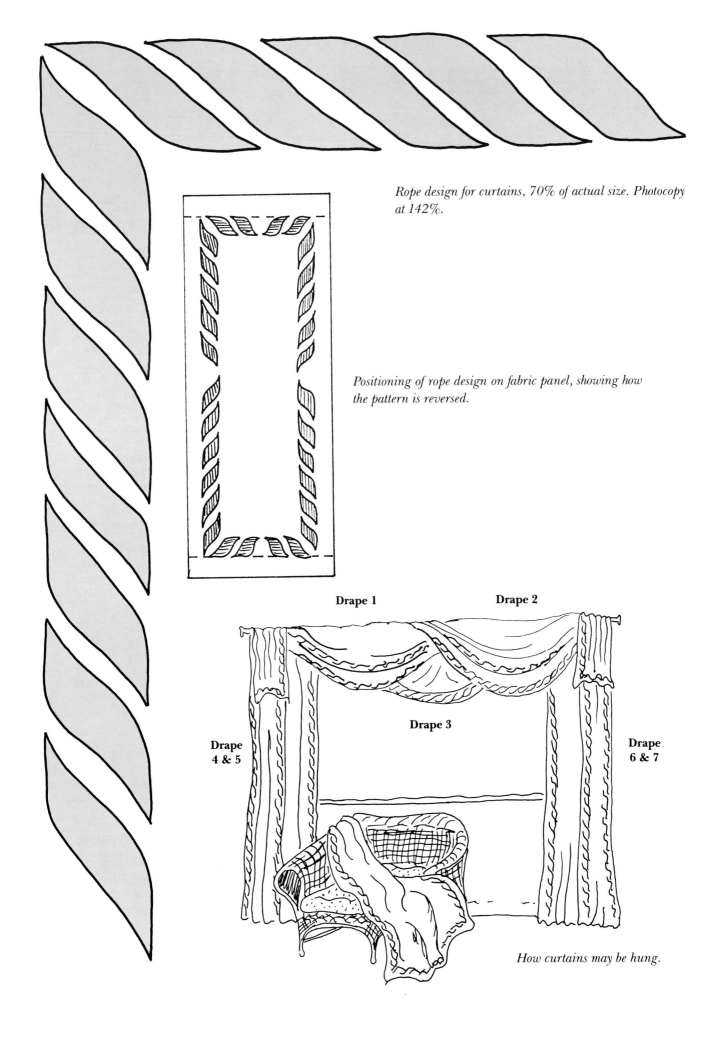

Rope design for curtains, 70% of actual size. Photocopy at 142%.

Positioning of rope design on fabric panel, showing how the pattern is reversed.

Drape 1   **Drape 2**

Drape 3

Drape 4 & 5

Drape 6 & 7

How curtains may be hung.

Picket Fence Curtain Ties and Throw Pillows

Curtain Ties

YOU WILL NEED*

❖ For each tieback: 14 inches (36 cm) × 6.5-inch (15 cm) piece of cotton fabric in your choice of color and pattern (I have used a checked gingham for fun)

❖ Basic supplies (see page 10)

❖ Iron-on interfacing about 14 × 3 inches (18 × 7.5 cm) for each tieback

❖ Polyester batting, 14 × 3 inches (18 × 7.5 cm) for each tieback (optional)

❖ Brass rings (2 for each tieback)

❖ Stencil: picket fence

❖ 1 roller

❖ White paint

*See the separate materials list for the throw pillows.

Adapt the tieback idea shown here to suit your own circumstances—the stencil can be as simple or ornate as you choose. For example, you could add a flower pattern along with the fence. Tiebacks can give a new look to an existing curtain, or they can be the finishing touch on a new window treatment; it's up to you.

1. Enlarge the curtain tieback pattern and cut out your fabric and interfacing pieces, following the curtain tieback pattern. The interfacing should be about ½ inch (1 cm) narrower than the fabric when folded on its length, as the edges of the fabric will become the seam allowances. The batting is the same size as the interfacing.

2. Carefully enlarge and cut out your fence stencil from drafting film and spray the back of the stencil lightly with spray adhesive to hold it firmly in place on the fabric.

3. Roll the paint onto the stencil as shown in the basics section of the book. Because I used white over the checked pattern, I needed to roll on a couple of layers of white paint to cover up the underlying fabric color, so I rolled the paint onto the fabric a little longer than usual. Don't be tempted to put more color on the roller in an attempt to cover the checks, however. If the paint is too thick, it will build up around the edges of the stencil and look untidy, or the paint will seep under the edges of the stencil and you will end up with a soggy mess.

4. When you have finished rolling on the paint and it is dry, remove the stencil; heat-set the paint as described in the basics section.

5. Iron the interfacing onto the wrong side of the painted tieback, with its fusible side facing the fabric.

6. Fold the tieback in half on its length, with right sides together. Baste in a layer of batting the same shape as the folded tieback, before you stitch, if you want a more sculptured look. This looks great if it is then quilted. Stitch around the edge with a ½-inch (1 cm) seam allowance, leaving one end open to turn the tieback right-side out.

7. Press the tieback with an iron and hand-stitch the turning opening closed.

8. Hand-stitch a small brass ring at each end of the tieback so you can hook it onto the window frame.

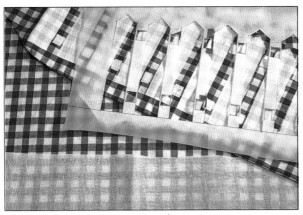

Closeup of tieback showing stencilling on gingham.

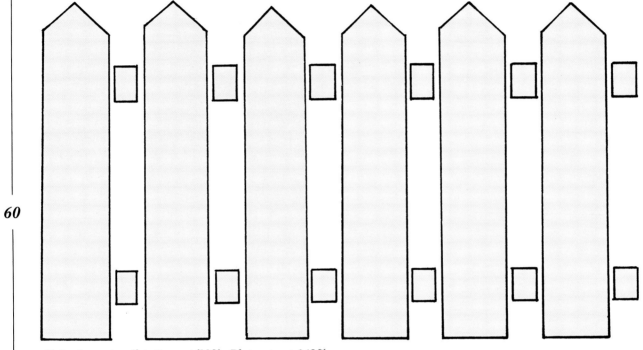

Picket fence stencil pattern at 70%. Photocopy at 142%.

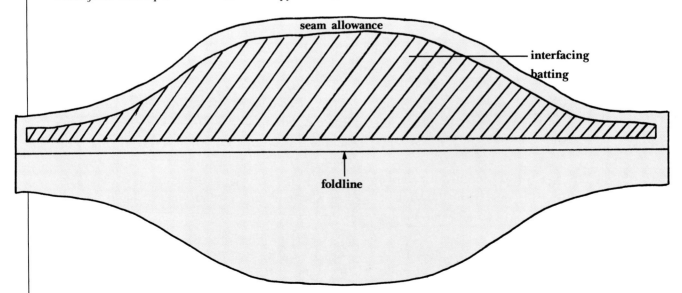

seam allowance

interfacing

batting

foldline

Pattern for curtain tieback (outer line) at 50%. Photocopy at 200%.

Sweet Pea Stencilled Throw Pillows

As you can see from the photo, I made one throw pillow with a sweet pea plus picket fence design and one with a sweet pea design alone; you can adapt the designs to suit yourself.

YOU WILL NEED

❖ Gingham fabric or other fabric (amount depends on the size of your throw pillows)

❖ Pillow forms (one for each throw pillow) if you are making new throw pillows

❖ Sweet pea and picket fence stencils

❖ Basic supplies (as for tieback)

❖ Paints: white, soft green, pink, lavender

The instructions to make up the throw pillows are the same for each throw pillow.

1. For each throw pillow, measure the size of the throw pillow front and add ⅝ inch (1.5 cm) seam allowance all around. Cut out the pillow front. Cut the back about 4 inches (10 cm) wider than the top (the length stays the same), then cut it into two pieces to provide an overlap through which to insert the pillow form or

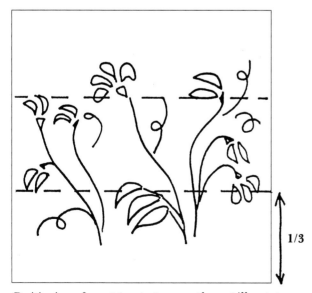

Positioning of sweet pea pattern on throw pillow top.

1/3

throw pillow (see diagrams with the Celtic Throw Pillows project, page 52).

2. Enlarge or reduce your stencil patterns according to your pillow size. Cut out your stencils from drafting film.

3. Spray the back of the stencils with a light spray of adhesive.

4. For each pillow, place the sweet pea stencil on the throw pillow top, with the lower edge of the stencil on the lower third of the pillow top (see diagram).

5. Stencil the leaves and stems green first; then paint all the flowers white; then overlay the flowers with pink and lavender. White takes longer than some other colors to dry, so be sure it is completely dry before overlaying the other colors.

6. For the pillow with the picket fence, place the picket fence stencil over the lower part of the flower stencil and paint it white.

7. Reposition the sweet pea stencil over the picket fence and repaint the leaves coming over the top of the fence in green.

8. Heat-set the paints with an iron when the paint is dry (see basic instructions).

9. Measure around the outside edge of the throw pillow top, and cut a strip of fabric twice the length and twice the width required for the finished ruffle; include seam allowances in your measurements. For a 2-inch-wide (5 cm wide) finished ruffle, cut a piece 5 inches (12.5 cm) wide; this includes 1 inch (2.5 cm) of seam allowance. Piece the fabric, if necessary, to make the ruffle as long as you need it.

10. Fold the ruffle in half lengthwise, right-side out, and press it flat.

11. Run two lines of basting stitches around the cut edge of the ruffle, ½ inch (1 cm) in from the cut edge, and pull them up to fit the ruffle around the edge of the throw pillow front. Pin and baste it in place around the front of the throw pillow on the right side of the pillow front with raw edges aligned and facing out.

Sweet pea stencil pattern, at 90%. Photocopy at 111%.

62

12. Set the throw pillow top aside. Hem the edges of the two parts of the back of the pillow where they will overlap with a small hem, about ⅝ inch (1.5 cm).

13. Pin the back pillow pieces to the pillow front, with the right sides of fabric facing the right side of the pillow front, keeping the ruffle facing in, overlapping the back pieces at the center. Machine-stitch the back to the front with a ⅝-inch seam allowance.

14. Trim the seam allowances narrower at the corners to reduce bulk; then turn the throw pillow cover right-side out.

15. Press the seams flat and push each throw pillow or pillow form into its cover. You can hand-sew the overlap at the back closed if you wish, or leave it open so the throw pillow can be easily removed to dry clean.

❖ ❖ ❖ ❖ ❖ ❖ ❖ ❖ ❖ ❖ ❖ ❖

Bathroom Towels and Washcloths

Stencilling on towelling is an interesting experience. Because of the texture of the surface, care is needed in applying the paint. Once you start stencilling, there will be a real temptation to load up the roller with lots of paint and go wild. *Resist the temptation!* Roll the excess paint off the roller (you may even prefer to try a brush on the towelling). It will take a lot longer to build up the desired color on towelling than it does on other fabrics, but your perseverance will pay off. Apply a bit more pressure than usual when you are stencilling to ensure that the paint gets through to the base of the pile.

If you decide to create your own designs to go on towelling, be careful not to choose one that has a lot of small detail; it will get lost in the texture of the towel. Larger, more chunky designs are better. (You can have more detailed designs on velvet-finished towels.)

YOU WILL NEED

❖ Selection of towels and matching washcloths

❖ Basic supplies (see page 10)

❖ One roller or brush for each color

❖ Stencils: Shells, anchors, bunch of flowers, elephants (pages 64–68)

❖ Paints: blue, red, white, black, yellow, apricot (light orange), burgundy (dark red), green

1. Enlarge and cut out your stencils from drafting film. Spray adhesive on the back of the stencil you want to use; you may need a little more than usual because of the pile on the surface, but not too much. It doesn't have to stay there for life, it is just there to hold the stencil in place while you work.

2. Mix the colors you need for the stencil you

are using (see the photos for guidance, or choose your own color combination). Be patient in applying the paint: it is worth the effort. If you put on too much paint, it becomes hard and scratchy, which is not good on a towel.

3. When you need to stencil a color on a dark background, first stencil the whole design in white paint. When the white has dried, apply the final color over the white. If the white isn't completely dry, the color you put on top will blend with the white and come out lighter.

4. For the spring flowers stencil, you will need to mask the previous colors you applied as you apply the new ones, to ensure that the colors come out nice and crisp and separate.

5. To stencil the washcloths, choose the section of the design that you want to use on the washcloth and mask off the rest. Then stencil the washcloths in the same way you stencilled the towels.

64

Bouquet pattern for bathroom towels, at 50% actual size. Photocopy at 200%.

Anchor pattern for bathroom towels, at 50% actual size.
Photocopy at 200%.

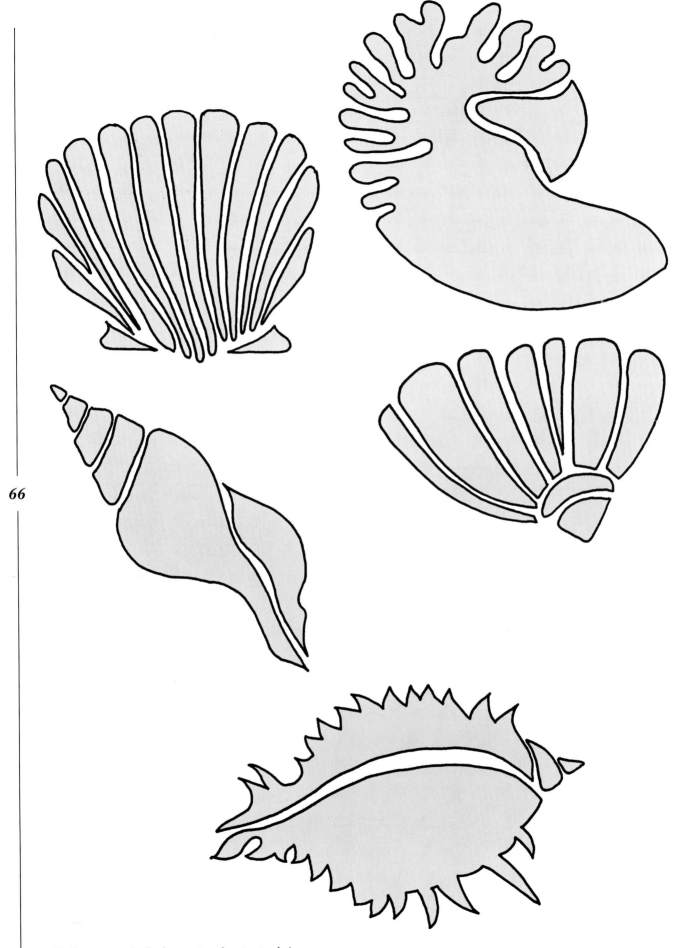

Shell patterns, for bathroom towels, at actual size.

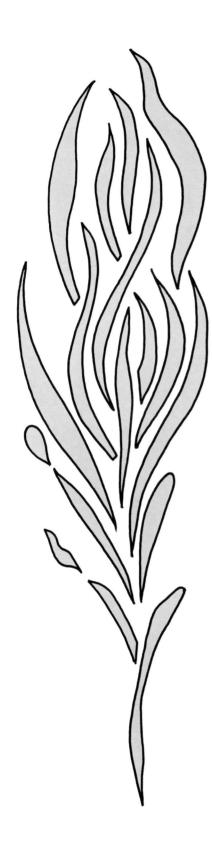

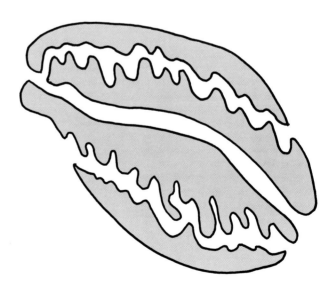

Shell and seaweed pattern for bathroom towels, at actual size.

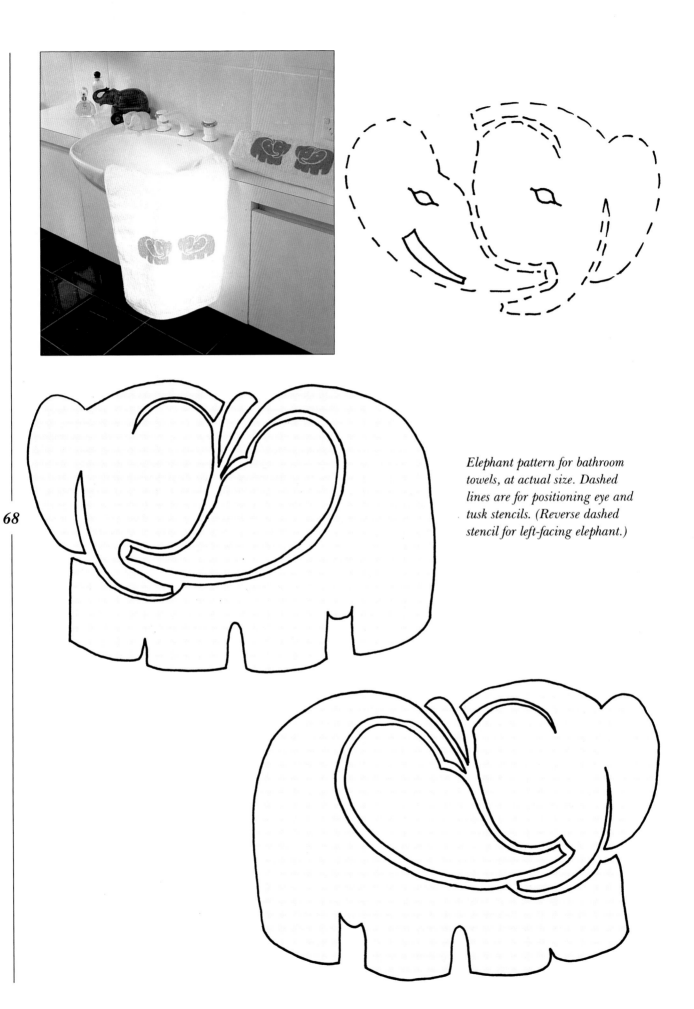

Elephant pattern for bathroom towels, at actual size. Dashed lines are for positioning eye and tusk stencils. (Reverse dashed stencil for left-facing elephant.)

Child's Floral Comforter Cover and Pillowcase

YOU WILL NEED

❖ White or other light-colored fabric (enough to make a blanket or comforter cover)*

❖ White or light-colored pillowcase (store-bought or homemade)

❖ Basic supplies (see page 10)

❖ Floral stencils (pages 70 and 71)

❖ Paints: magenta, green, medium yellow, phthalo blue

❖ Something to close the cover, such as Velcro fastening tape, snaps, ribbons, or hooks and eyes

*You may have to piece fabric to cover the wider sizes of comforter. Or make the cover out of two sheets that are large enough to cover the comforter with a few inches extra on each side for seam allowances and hems.

In the instructions below, you make up the cover first and then stencil it. You can stencil the comforter top before you make up the cover, however, mainly because the large amount of fabric to be painted makes it rather unwieldy to handle otherwise.

1. Cut two pieces of fabric, one for a comforter top and one for a comforter backing; each should extend a few inches wider on each side than your comforter, and have 3 or 4 inches extra at the top (open side) for a hem. Hem the edges of the fabric pieces that will be at the open end of the comforter cover, if they are not already hemmed.

2. With right sides of fabric facing, machine-stitch the cover top to the cover backing at the side seams and the bottom.

3. Stitch Velcro, snaps, ribbons, or some other closure devices onto the end of the cover that will not be sewn closed.

4. Press the seams and the fabric to remove the wrinkles.

5. Enlarge and cut out your stencils from drafting film. Plan the positioning of your stencils around the cover top, and mark their position with tailor's chalk or fabric marking pencil. If you are stencilling on the made-up cover, be sure to place cardboard or paper between the top and bottom layers of the fabric to avoid the color seeping through to the back of the cover. Lay the stencil along the edge of the cover, hold it in place with spray adhesive, and begin to stencil (see photo for reference). You will need a good coverage of paint to give nice, crisp colors. Because it is such a simple design, it looks best if the colors are separate, so mask off the completed colors' areas as you work, to protect them.

6. Stencil the pillowcase using the same colors you used in the comforter cover (see photo).

7. Heat-set the paints; because this is a large project, you may find it easier to put it into the clothes dryer for about 10 minutes on high to set the paints than to use an iron.

Flower pattern (one of two stencils) for floral comforter cover and pillowcase; 50% of actual size. Photocopy at 200%.

Flower pattern (second of two stencils) for floral comforter cover and pillowcase; 50% of actual size. Dashed line indicates where pattern 1 overlaps. Photocopy at 200%.

Jungle Lampshade and Comforter Cover

Another fun theme for a child's room is a jungle scene. Ask your son or daughter to draw pictures and translate them into stencils, or use the ones given in this project.

Lampshade

YOU WILL NEED*

❖ Lampshade and lamp base

❖ Basic supplies (see page 10)

❖ Stencil of jungle foliage (page 73)

❖ Paint: Red, yellow, blue, and black, to mix 5 different shades of green, as well as brown, yellow, and red

❖ Spray adhesive

*See additional supplies list for comforter cover.

1. After cutting out the lampshade stencil from drafting film, lay it on the lampshade to see how it fits. Because the shade's surface is a cone, the stencil is a bit more difficult to handle than it would be on a flat surface. You may need to trim down the border on the stencil to make it easier to handle.

2. Spray adhesive on the back of the stencil, using just a *little* bit more than usual, to ensure

that it stays in place. The entire stencil probably won't lie flat on the surface of the shade all at once, so, depending on how tapered the shade's curve is, you will need to stencil the design in a couple of stages. Adhere the leftmost part of the stencil onto the shade; let the rest sit loosely above the shade. Stencil the paints onto your shade in the adhered area. After that part has been stencilled, carefully press the rest of the stencil onto the shade, so that the part of the stencil that has already been painted lifts up. Continue adhering the stencil parts and stencilling the design until you have stencilled the whole design.

3. As you stencil your different colors, overlap and blend them to give texture to the jungle.

4. You don't need to heat-set the lampshade, because it will have plenty of heat on it each time the light is on, and you will not be washing it. Keep the dust off it so that it doesn't get too grubby.

Jungle Comforter Cover

YOU WILL NEED

❖ White or other light-colored fabric (enough to make a blanket cover or comforter cover)*

❖ White or light-colored pillowcase (store-bought or homemade)

❖ Basic supplies as for lampshade

❖ Jungle stencils (pages 74 and 75)

❖ Paints: same as for lampshade

❖ Something to close the cover, such as Velcro fastening tape, snaps, ribbons, or hooks and eyes

*You may have to piece fabric to cover the wider sizes of comforter. Or make the cover out of two sheets that are large enough to cover the comforter plus have a few inches extra on each side for seam allowances and hems.

Follow the instructions for the floral comforter cover (page 69), but use the jungle stencils instead of the floral stencils.

Pattern for jungle lampshade, at 75%. Photocopy at 133%.

Stencilling a shade. See text for details.

74

Pattern for jungle comforter cover (one of two stencils) at 66% of actual size. Photocopy at 150%. Dashed line indicates overlap with the second stencil.

Pattern for jungle comforter cover (second of two stencils) at 66% of actual size. Photocopy at 150%.

75

Geometric Dish Towels or Place Mats

YOU WILL NEED

❖ Linen or cotton dish towels or place mats

❖ Basic supplies (see page 10)

❖ Stencils (page 77)

❖ Paints: olive green, light yellow, medium yellow

1. Plan the designs for each towel. Cut the stencils out of drafting film. Put down a line of cellophane tape to align the stencils if necessary so they are straight.

2. Spray the back of each stencil with spray adhesive to adhere it to the towel while you work.

3. On abstract designs like these, it is better to separate the colors rather than blending them, so mask off the areas of the stencil that you don't want to receive paint as you work.

4. Do your stencilling, and let the paint dry.

5. Heat-set the paint. It is particularly critical that the paint be well set, as the towels or place mats will be washed regularly.

Ideas ❖❖❖❖❖❖❖❖❖❖❖❖❖❖❖

❖ Stencil geometric designs to match the towels on an apron or oven mitt.

Patterns for geometric tea towels, actual size.

77

Italian Fruit Bowl Tablecloth

There are many different variations to this theme; for example, you can make some napkins to match the cloth. This project makes a wonderful gift; it looks exotic and is inexpensive.

YOU WILL NEED

❖ Calico or other lightweight woven cotton fabric: enough to cover the tabletop, extend down to overhang the side, and turn a hem, plus extra for napkins if desired

❖ Basic supplies for stencilling (see page 10)

❖ Stencils: Fruit, bowl and leaf (p. 79 and 80)

❖ Paints: green, purple, red, peach, yellow ochre

❖ 5 rollers

1. Cut out the stencils from drafting film. Spray the back of each stencil with spray-on adhesive as you need to use the stencil.

2. Iron the fabric to remove any wrinkles. Stencil the bowls in the corners of the tablecloth in ochre. Use a fabric marking pencil to plan the spacing of more bowls around the edge of the cloth and stencil them at equal intervals. If the tablecloth is circular or oval, stencil the bowls at equal intervals at least 3 or 4 inches (7 to 10 cm) in from the edge (remember to leave room for a hem).

3. Position the fruit stencil over the painted bowl and stencil the fruit, allowing the colors in the fruit to blend. Repeat for all the bowls.

4. In the center of the cloth, stencil the fruit only; reverse the fruit stencil to create the fruit garland (see closeup photo).

6. Using the leaf stencil, stencil small green leaves, scattered all over the tablecloth.

7. Heat-set all the paints (see general instructions).

8. Hem the edges of the tablecloth.

9. Make matching napkins if you like.

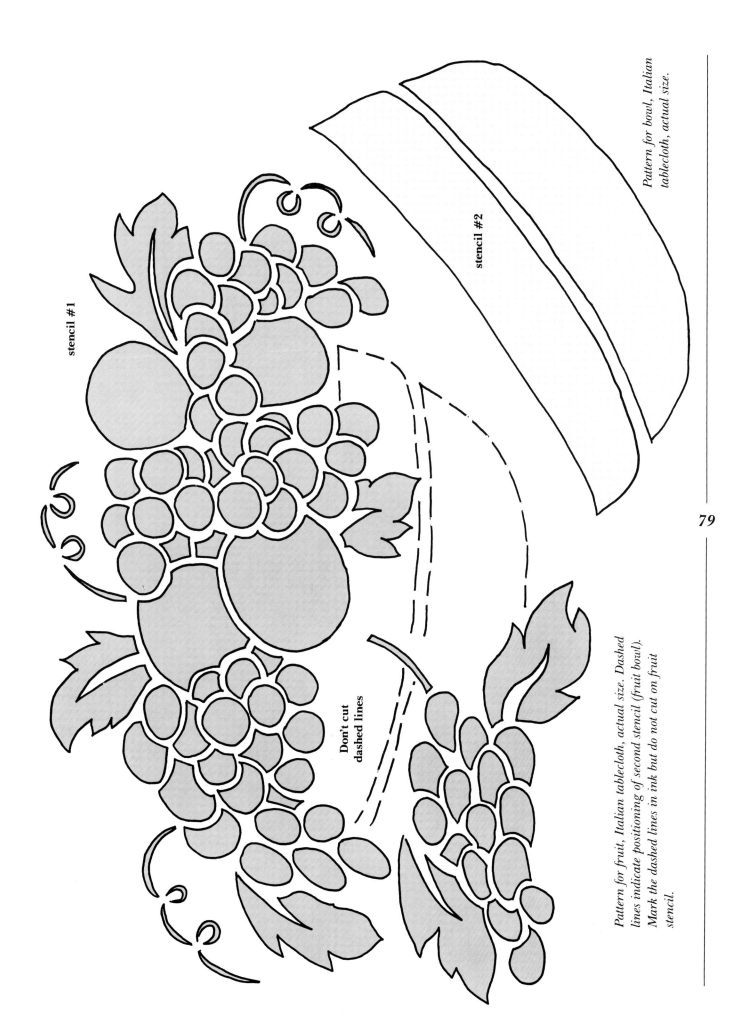

stencil #1

stencil #2

Don't cut
dashed lines

Pattern for fruit, Italian tablecloth, actual size. Dashed lines indicate positioning of second stencil (fruit bowl). Mark the dashed lines in ink but do not cut on fruit stencil.

Pattern for bowl, Italian tablecloth, actual size.

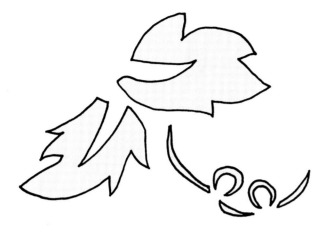

Children's Designs

Children can be demanding creatures. Although we love them very much, satisfying their whims and wishes can be very expensive. As a result, parents are always looking for ways to make unique clothes at reasonable prices. As suggested earlier for quilt covers and curtains, you can use designs adapted from children's own drawings, or the latest craze or logo, to try to fill the "bottomless pit." You can stencil on ready-made clothes or on ones you sew yourself.

The projects in this section show clothes for young children, but the ideas can be adapted to any age group. These ideas are just to get you started; once you see the possibilities, there will be no stopping you. If you have any questions about the basic instructions, refer to the basic section of the book; the details of some of the how-to parts have been abbreviated here, as they were described earlier.

When you look for ready-made clothes to stencil, buy ones made of natural fibers; synthetics don't absorb the paint as well as cottons and wools. Synthetics can be quite successfully painted, but the paints tend to sit on the surface, rather than soak into the fibers. When heat-setting the paint, use a cotton pressing cloth over the top of the synthetic fabric, so that you can make the iron hot enough to set the stencilled paint without burning or melting the fabric. A large handerchief or a piece of calico will serve as a pressing cloth. (See the fabric section for more information about specific fabrics.)

Choose clothes that are solid colored, or in patterns that will complement your stencil design. Stripes or checks can look great with a bumblebee or a snake climbing up a ladder stencilled onto them.

The area to be stencilled should to be easy to get to, and the stencil has to be a suitable size for the area. For instance, if you want to stencil on a sleeve, you need to be able to fit the stencil onto the sleeve and to be able to apply paint effectively. Be careful to paint on the right side of the fabric, and if the design is over an area with a seam in it, that seam will need to be stitched before painting. You may need to reduce stencil sizes on clothing for small children.

Washability of clothes that are stencilled is also an important consideration, as children are renowned for dropping things on their clothes. Stencilled designs can be washed, but soaking or spot scrubbing is not recommended. Most paints will withstand this sort of cleaning, but the chances of their rubbing or soaking off are quite good. It is better to use paints that are manufactured as fabric paints for children's clothes, rather than paints that require the addition of a textile medium to make them adhere to fabric.

When making up the clothes yourself, always stencil them before sewing them together. It is much easier to paint on a flat piece of fabric than on something that is gathered or has seams in it.

There are unlimited ideas as to what you can do with a T-shirt, a stencil and some paints. You can use any of the designs in the book, or try a children's coloring book for designs. You can also apply any of these designs to socks, bibs, or hats.

❖ ❖ ❖ ❖ ❖ ❖ ❖ ❖ ❖ ❖ ❖ ❖

Frog Sweatshirt

YOU WILL NEED

❖ Stencils of tree frog
❖ Basic supplies (see page 10)
❖ Sweatshirt: dark green or another color
❖ Paints: light green, yellow, light brown
❖ 3 rollers

1. Place a piece of cardboard in between the back and the front of the sweatshirt top.
2. Cut out the stencils from drafting film. Spray the back of stencil #1 with adhesive and position the stencil so it is centered just below the neckline. If you place it too low, it sits on the stomach and disappears when the wearer sits down.
3. Paint the frog green with a yellow tummy and light brown branch. Keep the colors light to contrast with the dark green of the sweatshirt. If the colors are too dark, they will not be seen. Do the details of the frog's body (stencil #2) last.
4. Heat-set the paints (see the general instructions).

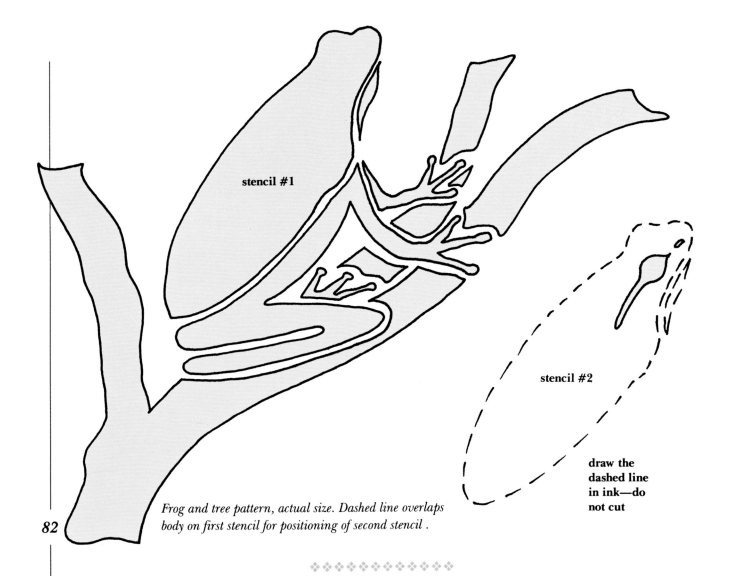

stencil #1

stencil #2

draw the dashed line in ink—do not cut

Frog and tree pattern, actual size. Dashed line overlaps body on first stencil for positioning of second stencil.

❖❖❖❖❖❖❖❖❖❖❖❖

Overalls with Engine Stencil

YOU WILL NEED

❖ 1 pair of chambray (lightweight denim) overalls

❖ 2 red buttons (optional)

❖ Train stencils

❖ Basic supplies (see page 10)

❖ Paints: blue, red, white

❖ Three rollers

If you sew your own overalls, it's easier to stencil the design before sewing the parts together.

1. Cut out the stencils from drafting film. Draw the dashed line on stencil #2 in ink; it is a guideline for positioning stencil #2 over stencil #1.

2. Lay stencil #1 on the bib or pocket and paint; put a piece of cardboard in the pocket and behind the bib to protect the fabric beneath. The face and smoke were cut as two separate stencils. Paint the face with dark blue after the train paint has dried. Paint the smoke white.

3. Heat-set the paints (see general instructions).

4. Sew on the red buttons for decoration.

Closeup shows how stencils were cut.

stencil #3

Stencil #2

draw the dashed line in ink—do not cut

83

stencil #1

Engine patterns, actual size. Make separate stencils for the features of the face (circle) and the smoke. Dashed line is drawn in ink (not cut) for registration.

Jumper Dress

YOU WILL NEED

❖ Ready-made jumper dress, or pattern and fabric to make one

❖ Rose stencils: garland and bunch of roses (pages 85 and 86)

❖ Basic supplies (see page 10)

❖ Paints: pink, blue, green

❖ 3 rollers

If you are sewing the dress yourself, stencil the designs on before assembling the dress. See general instructions for positioning patterns, especially the part about sizing stencils and positioning a repeat pattern for a border.

1. Enlarge or reduce the stencil patterns if necessary so that they will fit well on the size of dress you have. Cut out the stencils from drafting film.

2. Fold the dress bib in half vertically and press it to mark the center front of the bib. Use the pressed line as a guide for centering the bow on the bunch of flowers. Stencil the bunch of roses onto the bib of the dress.

3. Mark a line with cellophane tape or tailor's chalk to guide you for positioning the stencils around the skirt of the dress. Position the bow in the garland so that it is in the center front of the skirt, and work around the skirt from there, creating a garland effect. Leave space below the stencil for the hem of the skirt. Mask off each color as you go.

4. Heat-set the paint.

Garland pattern for jumper dress, actual size.

Bouquet pattern for jumper dress, actual size.

Sailing Ship T-Shirt

adhesive on the back of the stencil and position it on the T-shirt. Be careful when laying it on so that the shirt doesn't stretch and distort under the stencil.

3. Apply white paint onto the sails and the water. You will need to apply a couple of layers of paint; otherwise you will end up with pink sails with the red showing through the white. Don't be tempted to make the white paint too thick all at once; it will be ugly and thick and will creep under the edges of the stencil. Build up the color slowly with thin layers.

4. Paint the ship brown; then highlight the waves with blue.

5. White paint tends to stay sticky longer than other colors, so be sure that the paint is well and truly dry before ironing it to heat-set it.

YOU WILL NEED

- ❖ Red T-shirt
- ❖ Basic supplies (see page 10)
- ❖ Stencil of sailing ship
- ❖ Paints: white, brown, blue
- ❖ Three rollers

When you are stencilling on a fabric that has a stretch to it, like ribbed knits or Lycra®, be careful not to put too much pressure on the roller. If you do, it will stretch the fabric and distort the design.

1. Place a piece of cardboard between the layers of the T-shirt.

2. Cut out the stencil from drafting film. Spray

Sailing ship pattern, actual size.

88

Balloon Sweatshirt

YOU WILL NEED

- ❖ Blue sweatshirt
- ❖ Basic supplies (see page 10)
- ❖ Balloon stencil
- ❖ Paints: white, red, green, yellow, light blue
- ❖ 5 rollers

1. Place a piece of cardboard between the layers of the shirt.

2. Cut out the stencil from drafting film. Spray adhesive on the back of the stencil and position it on the shirt.

3. Paint the whole stencil with a few layers of white paint. A couple of white layers are necessary to block off the dark blue background so you will get nice, clear colors for the balloons.

4. When the white has completely dried, paint each individual balloon in red, yellow, green, or blue (see the photograph for guidance). Mask off places you don't want paint to go, as you work.

5. Heat-set the paints when they are dry (see general instructions).

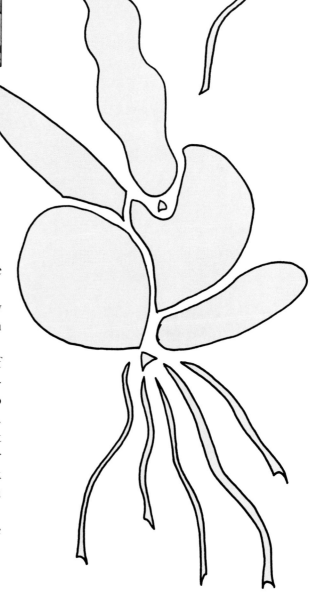

89

Layette

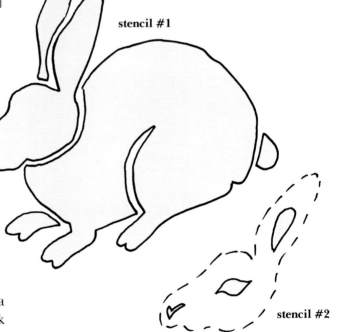

YOU WILL NEED

❖ Baby jumpsuit (stretch 1-piece garment)

❖ Terry-cloth pants

❖ Undershirts (vests)

❖ Bib

❖ Basic supplies (see page 10)

❖ Bunny and flower stencils

❖ Paints: aqua, dark aqua, green, orange

❖ 4 rollers

Protect the back of each garment by putting a piece of cardboard between the front and back layers before you start to stencil.

1. Cut the stencils out of drafting film. For the undershirts: Place the stencil close to the neckline, after having sprayed the back with spray adhesive. Be careful when placing the stencil that the ribs in the undershirt don't stretch.

2. Stencil the body of the bunny in light aqua on the shirt, jumpsuit, and pants; then stencil the eye, ear, and nose separately in the dark aqua when the body paint is dry.

3. Paint the flowers—do the green leaves first, then the orange flowers.

4. Heat-set all the paints when they are dry (see general instructions).

stencil #1

stencil #2

stencil #3

Bunny and flower patterns for layette, actual size. Make a second stencil for the facial features and align with dashed line, which is drawn in ink, not cut, on the stencil.

Mother and Daughter Pansy T-Shirts

YOU WILL NEED

- ❖ White T-shirts
- ❖ Basic supplies (see page 10)
- ❖ Pansy stencils*
- ❖ Paints: purple, magenta, yellow, green
- ❖ 4 rollers

*The stencil on the child's shirt is 70% of the size of the adult stencil; apart from the size, they are the same. Reduce the design for the child's T-shirt on a photocopier before you cut the stencil film for the child's shirt.

1. Cut out your stencils from drafting film. Place a piece of cardboard between the layers of the T-shirt to protect the back.

2. Spray the back of the stencils with spray adhesive and position the stencils on the fronts of their respective shirts.

3. Mask off each of the colors as you stencil them to keep them separate (see general instructions about masking). Each flower has a yellow center.

4. Heat-set the paints after they are dried (see general instructions).

92

*Pattern for pansies. Use at this size
for woman's T-shirt; photocopy at
70% for child's shirt.*

Mother and Daughter Umbrella T-Shirt and Dress

open umbrella design, as well as the rain, in white to mask the dark color of the fabric. You may need to do more than one layer of white to keep the dark background from showing through.

3. When the white paint is dry, stencil the red and yellow on the umbrella, and the silver on the raindrops. Be sure the white is quite dry before applying the red and yellow, or they will end up pink and lemon!

4. Stencil the closed umbrella on the back of the shirt and dress in white first, and then in red and yellow.

5. After all the paints are dry, heat-set them (see general instructions).

YOU WILL NEED

❖ Black or navy blue T-shirt and child's dress

❖ Basic supplies (see page 10)

❖ Umbrella and raindrops stencils

❖ Paints: white, red, yellow, silver

❖ 4 rollers

1. Cut the stencils out of drafting film. Place a piece of cardboard between the layers of the T-shirt and between the layers of the dress to protect the back layer while you stencil.

2. On the garment's front, stencil the whole

First layers of paint are done in white.

*Pattern for front of umbrella
T-shirt and dress. Use at this
size for woman's T-shirt;
photocopy at 70% for the
child's dress.*

*Pattern for back of umbrella
T-shirt and dress, actual size.*

Fashion Designs

Fortunately, people have many choices when it comes to clothing styles these days, as they do in interior design styles. We can wear pretty much what we like, from miniskirts to long skirts, and tight T-shirts to oversize T-shirts. Some aspects change each season, but generally speaking, anything goes.

In this chapter, the intention is not to create stencilled clothes, but to give you an alternative to expensive designer clothes and the option of creating something unique. An evening jacket, hand-stencilled fabrics to cut and sew, and superb stencilled silk scarves and shawls are just a few possibilities.

Most people conjure up a picture of brightly colored clothes with huge patterns on them, like Hawaiian shirts, when you mention stencilled or screen-printed clothes. Stencilled fashions need not be bright or large; those of us who like smart and subtle colors will find that stencilling is an easy way of getting exactly the ones we want. You can have the best of both worlds; because the costs are reduced so much, you can have both bright and breezy and soft and subtle clothing. That is the beauty of stencilling. Furthermore, instead of spending hours running around looking for the perfectly patterned fabric to match a certain skirt of pair of pants, you can stencil a design in whatever color combination you like, either on fabric to make up into a shirt, for example, or on an already-made garment.

Stencilling is very similar to, and actually is the basis of, screen printing. Stencilling can achieve the same result without using toxic paints, setting up screens, and all the other problems associated with screen printing. Stencilling enables you to achieve much more subtle effects with the paints; by shading and blending colors, you can create movement in the design, which is very important on clothes that need to move and flow. Screen printing has a somewhat more rigid and flat appearance, which can tend to stay still while you move around inside the garment.

For choice of garments, you are not restricted to T-shirts and sweatsuits; you can revamp a favorite garment, or create a whole new outfit. The designs can be conservative or outrageous. You can find a stencil to suit any age. That is the beauty of this art: no one need be excluded.

All of the designs in this section are for women, but that doesn't mean that stencilling is restricted to women's clothes. T-shirts are perfect for men; club logos are great on polo shirts, as well as on boxer shorts; and you can create some amazing neckties, for starters, great gifts for that man who is difficult to shop for.

The main rule of stencilling is: "Try everything and anything." You can discover all sorts of new ideas by playing with designs and paints. As with all other areas of stencilling, practice your ideas on paper first, to give yourself some idea of how the finished garment will look, remembering that the paint will react slightly differently on the paper than on fabric.

Sometimes, if it is a particularly important project, it is a good idea to make it up in inexpensive calico first to get your fit, colors, and details right, before you move on to silk, wool, or other, more expensive fabrics. This all takes time, which unfortunately is something none of us have enough of, but it can be well worth the effort.

Heart T-Shirt

YOU WILL NEED

- ❖ White T-shirt
- ❖ Heart stencil
- ❖ Basic supplies (see page 10)
- ❖ Paint: mint green
- ❖ 1 roller

1. Cut the stencil out of drafting film. Spray adhesive the back of the stencil and center it high on the front of the T-shirt.

2. Place cardboard between the front and back of the T-shirt to protect the back.

3. Stencil carefully, without using too much paint. Apply a couple of layers to achieve all-over coverage with the paint.

4. Heat-set the paint with your iron when it is dry. If you are doing a number of T-shirts at once, put them in the clothes dryer on hot for 10 minutes to heat-set instead.

Pattern for heart T-shirt, actual size.

Bodysuit with Flowers

YOU WILL NEED

❖ Black bodysuit

❖ Basic supplies (page 10)

❖ Sunflowers stencil (page 98)

❖ Paints: red, yellow, gold, green, white

❖ Small translucent yellow and red glass beads

❖ 4 rollers

1. Enlarge the pattern and cut the stencil out of drafting film. Position the stencil around the curve of the neckline (see photo).

2. If you stencil your bright colors directly on the black background, you will end up with soft colors. If you want clear, bright colors, paint the entire stencil design onto the black background in white first (you may need to use several layers before it keeps the black from showing through); let the white paint dry; and then stencil the designs in the individual colors.

3. Heat-set the paints (see the general instructions).

4. Stitch beads onto the design to highlight the colors. In the model the centers of the flowers have been beaded with red and yellow beads.

Stitch glass beads in these areas after painting.

Pattern for sunflowers on bodysuit, at 88%. Photocopy at 113%.

Denim Vest with Sun

This design could be reduced and painted onto a pair of jeans as well, for a total look. The moon and stars stencil (page 100) carries out the celestial theme.

YOU WILL NEED

❖ Denim vest

❖ Sun stencil

❖ Basic supplies (see page 10)

❖ Paint: gold

❖ 1 roller

Sun pattern for denim vest, actual size.

1. Enlarge the pattern and cut the stencil out of drafting film. After spraying the back of the stencil with spray adhesive, position the stencil on the back of the vest.

2. Paint the sun on the vest with the gold paint. Several thin layers of the gold will mask the blue of the denim. It is better not to use white paint under the gold to mask the denim, because the white tends to make the metallic gold sit on the denim fibers, rather than soaking in.

3. Heat-set the paint when it is dry (see general instructions).

100

Moon and stars, actual size. May be used for denim vest or as desired.

Poppy Dress

YOU WILL NEED

- ❖ Calico dress
- ❖ Poppy stencil
- ❖ Basic supplies (see page 10)
- ❖ Paints: magenta, green
- ❖ 2 rollers

The skirt of the dress was made in panels, so I placed the stencil on each panel to give the effect of a garland. If the dress or skirt doesn't have panels, position the first stencil in the center of the front and work the stencil around to the back to create the same effect (see section on positioning of stencils on a circle in the basic instructions). The dark color in the centers of the flowers and on parts of the leaves is made by overlapping the green and magenta.

1. Enlarge and cut out the stencil from drafting film.

2. Make the belt from a piece of calico 45 inches (114 cm) × 7.5 inches (19 cm)—this is wide enough to fit the design and turn under a small hem on either long side of the fabric and on the ends. Position the stencil in the center of the fabric after you have hemmed it. The belt can be simply knotted at the back.

3. Stencil the poppy design in the center front of the belt.

4. Heat-set the paints when they are dry (see general instructions).

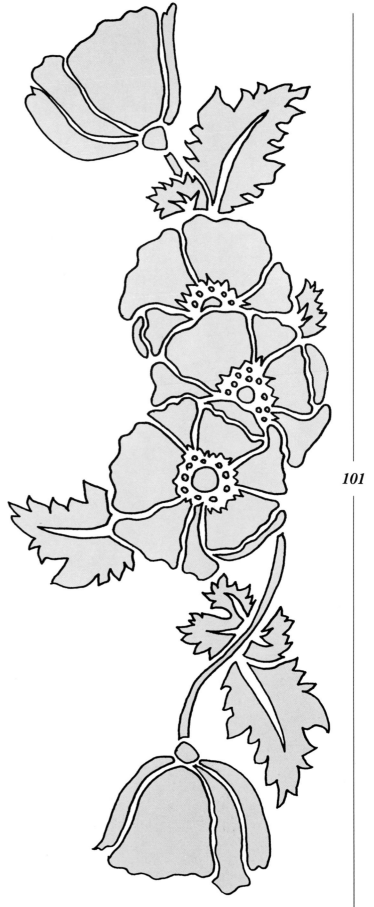

Poppy pattern for dress, 70% of actual size. Photocopy at 142%.

Woollen Cape

Front of the cape.

1. Enlarge and cut out your stencil from drafting film.

2. In the center back, I used the full stencil to create the symmetrical design (see photo).

3. Work the paint well into the wool surface. You will need to roll longer, with more paint, than you would on cotton to achieve the depth of color. Be careful that the paint doesn't become blobby on the wool as it catches the fibers. Continue to work the roller back and forth to achieve a nice, even finish.

4. Heat-set the paints well when they are dry, using a pressing cloth over the stencilled area, with the iron set to cotton.

Back of cape, showing design made by using full stencil pattern.

YOU WILL NEED

❖ Woollen cape

❖ Basic supplies (page 10)

❖ Aztec stencil

❖ Paints: red, yellow

❖ 2 rollers

This is a very simple design that is lined up end to end around the front of the cape (see photo), for which part of the design is masked (see stencil pattern). You can continue the design around the bottom edge as well if you choose.

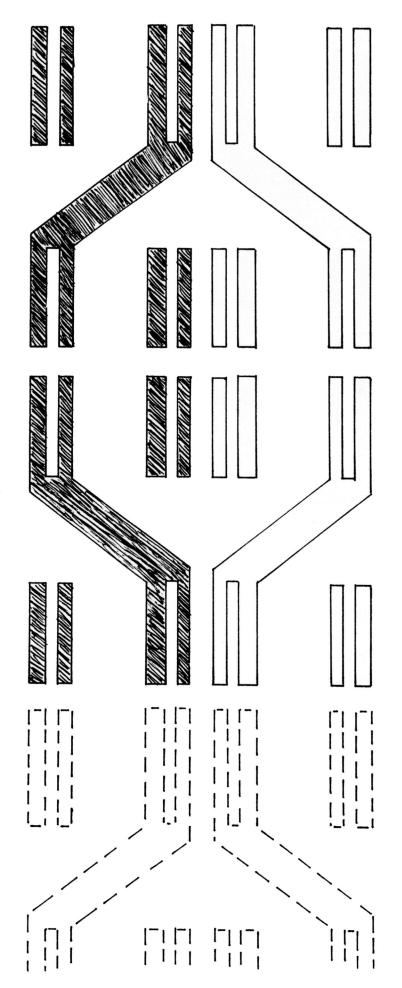

Stencil design at 56% of actual size. Photocopy at 178% to get full size. Hatched area is masked when you stencil the front edge, but used for the center back design. Dashed lines indicate position of pattern repeat.

Braided Suit

3. Remove the paper backing from the stencil film and position the stencil on the jacket pocket.
4. Stencil the design with gold paint. Repeat the process on the pocket of the trousers, so that the design is parallel to the pocket opening.
5. For the sleeves, mask the ends of the design, as shown on the stencil pattern.
6. Stuff the sleeve with paper towels so that the sleeve is filled and rounded; then place the stencil design on the sleeve, lining the stencil up with the edge and taking into consideration where the new button will go.
7. Stencil the sleeves.
8. Heat-set the paints.
9. Replace the buttons with gold buttons.

YOU WILL NEED

❖ Old suit
❖ Knot stencil
❖ Basic supplies (see page 10)
❖ Adhesive-backed stencil film
❖ Paint: gold
❖ 1 roller
❖ Gold buttons to replace existing buttons

Read the special instructions for stencilling and heat-setting on the fabric that your suit is made of in the Fabric section of the book.

1. Remove all the old buttons from the suit.
2. Transfer the design onto the stencil film and cut out the stencil, leaving the protective paper backing on the film.

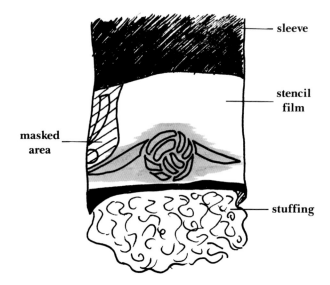

Stuff the sleeve before stencilling.

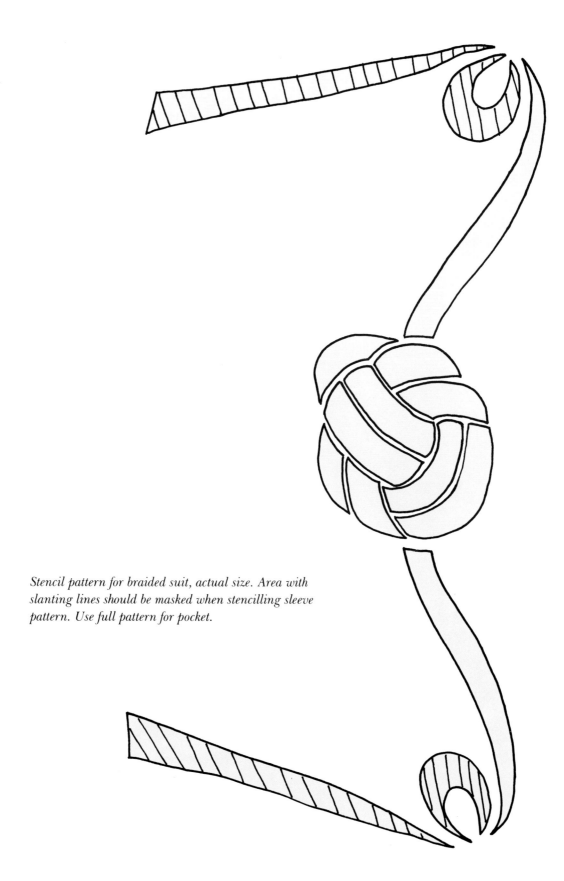

Stencil pattern for braided suit, actual size. Area with slanting lines should be masked when stencilling sleeve pattern. Use full pattern for pocket.

Tone-on-Tone Suit

YOU WILL NEED

❖ Suit made of shiny fabric, such as satin

❖ Basic supplies (see page 10)

❖ Stencils (pages 108 and 109)

❖ Paint: match color of fabric, plus gold

❖ 2 rollers

This simple embossing technique can be used on almost any kind of fabric, but works particularly well on a shiny fabric like satin or silk. The secret is making sure the paint color matches the fabric exactly. While you don't achieve a radical change in the garment, it is very subtle. The painted surface catches the light and gives a dramatic look.

1. Plan the design for the collar and pants yoke or jacket back of your suit; adapt the stencil patterns if necessary, including enlarging or reducing them as needed, and cut out the stencils from drafting film.

2. Stencil the design onto the collar of the jacket with the color of paint that matches the fabric, and highlight the design with a light application of gold paint. (If you are sewing your own suit, stencil the designs before making up the jacket.)

3. Stencil the yoke design onto the yoke of the trousers (if there is one) or onto the back of the jacket, being sure to center the design on the center of the garment.

4. Heat-set the paint using a piece of cotton fabric over the painted areas with the iron set on a high enough setting to set the paint. Be careful not to place the very hot iron directly onto the fabric as it will scorch.

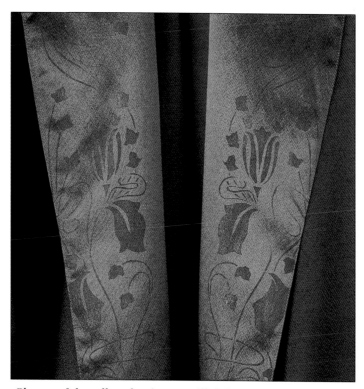

Closeup of the collar, showing stencilled designs.

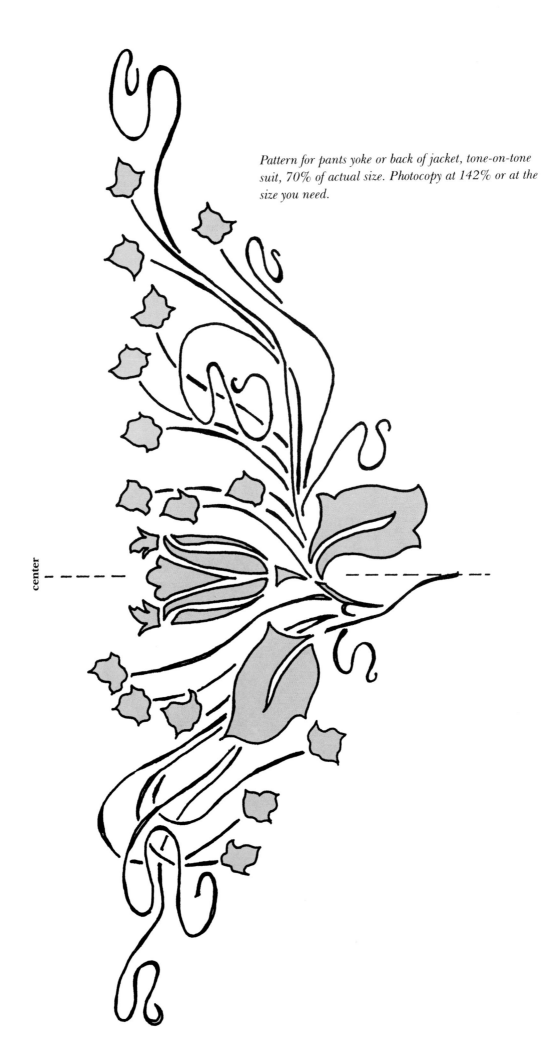

Pattern for pants yoke or back of jacket, tone-on-tone suit, 70% of actual size. Photocopy at 142% or at the size you need.

center

part 1

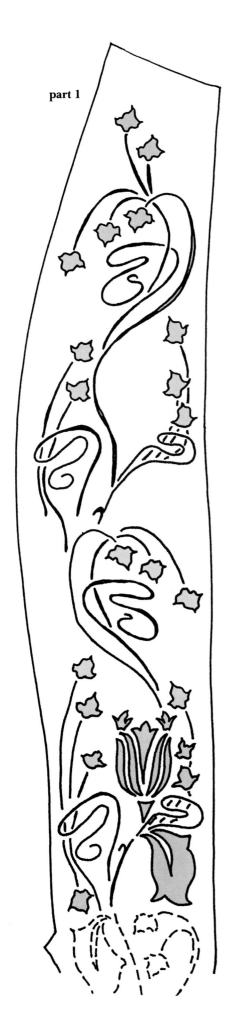

part 2

Patterns for collar of jacket, tone-on-tone suit, at 50%. Photocopy at 200%, or as needed. Use part or all of design, depending on the space you have to fill. Dashed line indicates where pattern pieces overlap to join.

"Lace" Dress

YOU WILL NEED

- ❖ Dark-colored dress
- ❖ Lace stencil pattern
- ❖ Basic supplies (see page 10)
- ❖ Paints: silver, gold
- ❖ 2 rollers

1. Measure the top of the dress bodice and enlarge the stencil pattern so that it will fit well on your dress. The idea is to make the stencil look like a lace overlay.

2. Cut out the stencil from drafting film. Put a piece of cardboard between the front and back layers of the dress, so that the paint won't seep through from the front to the back layer.

3. Stencil the design with silver paint; then for a contrast, lightly stencil over the silver around the edges of the flowers with gold paint (see closeup photo).

4. Heat-set the paint with a piece of cotton fabric over the painted area. This is particularly important if your fabric is a synthetic, as it will burn easily if the iron is too hot. See the fabric section of the book for details of the particular fabric you have chosen.

Closeup of "lace," showing gold highlights.

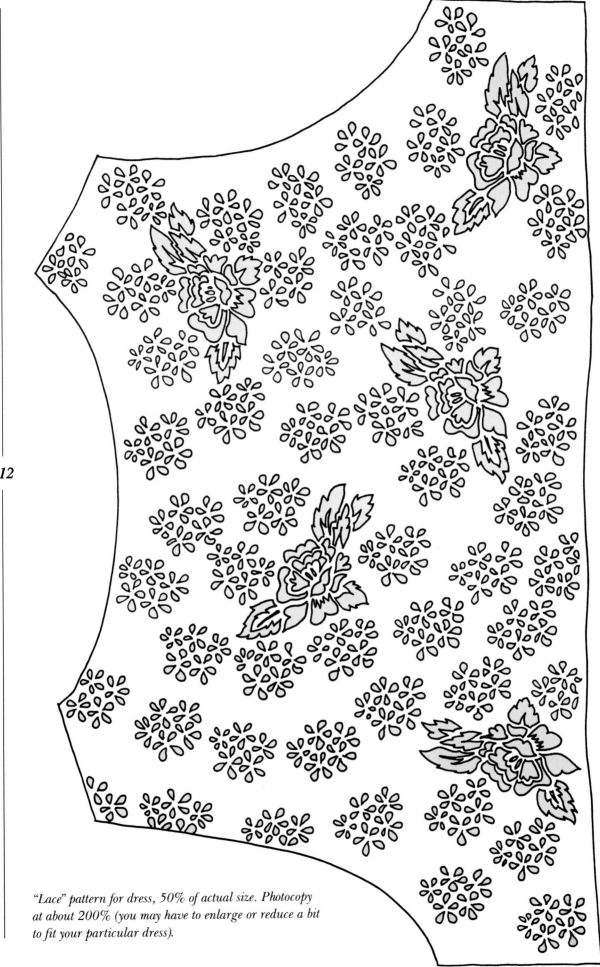

112

"Lace" pattern for dress, 50% of actual size. Photocopy at about 200% (you may have to enlarge or reduce a bit to fit your particular dress).

Fish Shirt

YOU WILL NEED

❖ White voile or other fine cotton shirt

❖ Fish and seaweed stencil patterns (pages 114–117)

❖ Basic supplies (see page 10)

❖ Paints: aqua, sapphire blue, green, black, burnt sienna

❖ 5 rollers

This makes a lovely shirt to wear over a swim-suit to keep the sun off—you could even paint the fish onto your swimsuit to match. Why not stencil a towel and beach bag also? Stencils of fish are given. There are also layouts, showing the positioning of the stencils on the seaweed. Dashed lines indicate the positioning of second stencils. Enlarge the stencils to a size that works well for the shirt you have and cut them from drafting film.

You can quite easily use the same basic idea with many other stencil designs. A branch of leaves and blossoms would look lovely draped over the shoulder of a shirt instead of the fish motif (see stencil pattern on page 142).

1. This design is easier to apply before the shirt is made up, but can be painted onto a ready-made shirt. If you're using an already-made garment, protect the layer of fabric behind the layer you're stencilling by putting a piece of cardboard in between to keep paint from seeping through where you don't want it.

2. Stencil one fish and seaweed on the right front panel of the shirt (see photo).

3. Arrange the fish and seaweed on the back of the shirt so that they are not all swimming the same way and so that they look as though they are swimming. You can create interesting effects by letting colors blend into each other in some areas, such as the fins, rather than keeping them masked off from each other.

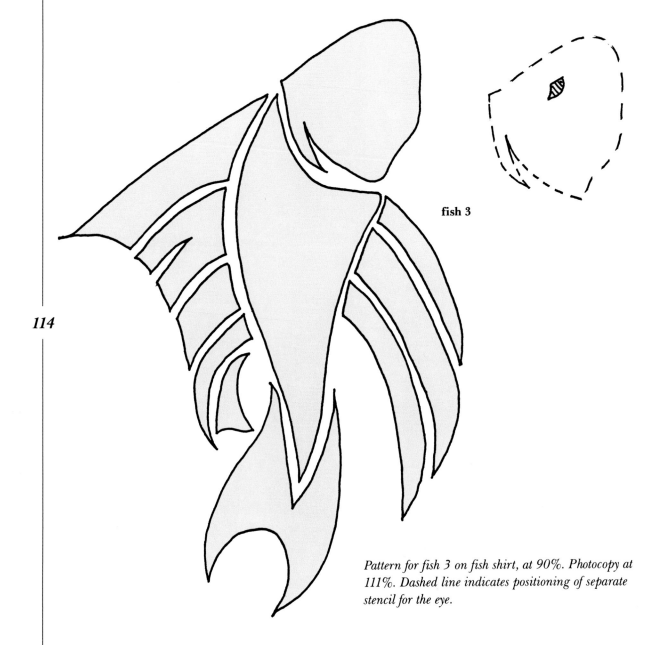

fish 3

Pattern for fish 3 on fish shirt, at 90%. Photocopy at 111%. Dashed line indicates positioning of separate stencil for the eye.

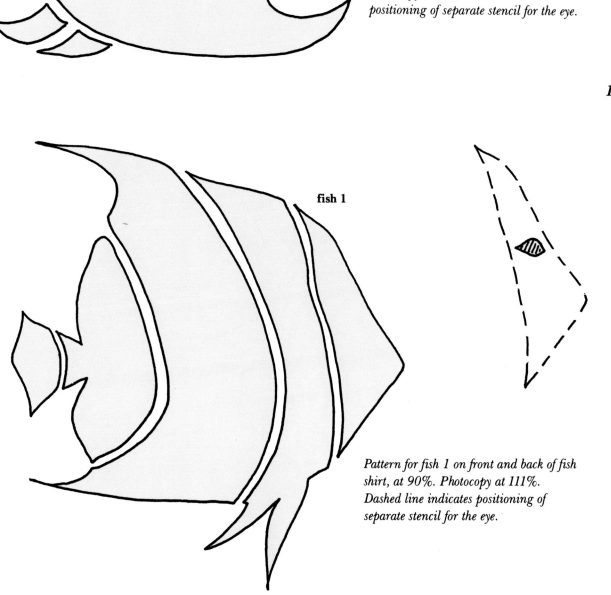

fish 2

Pattern for fish 2 on fish shirt, at 90%.
Photocopy at 111%. Dashed line indicates
positioning of separate stencil for the eye.

fish 1

Pattern for fish 1 on front and back of fish
shirt, at 90%. Photocopy at 111%.
Dashed line indicates positioning of
separate stencil for the eye.

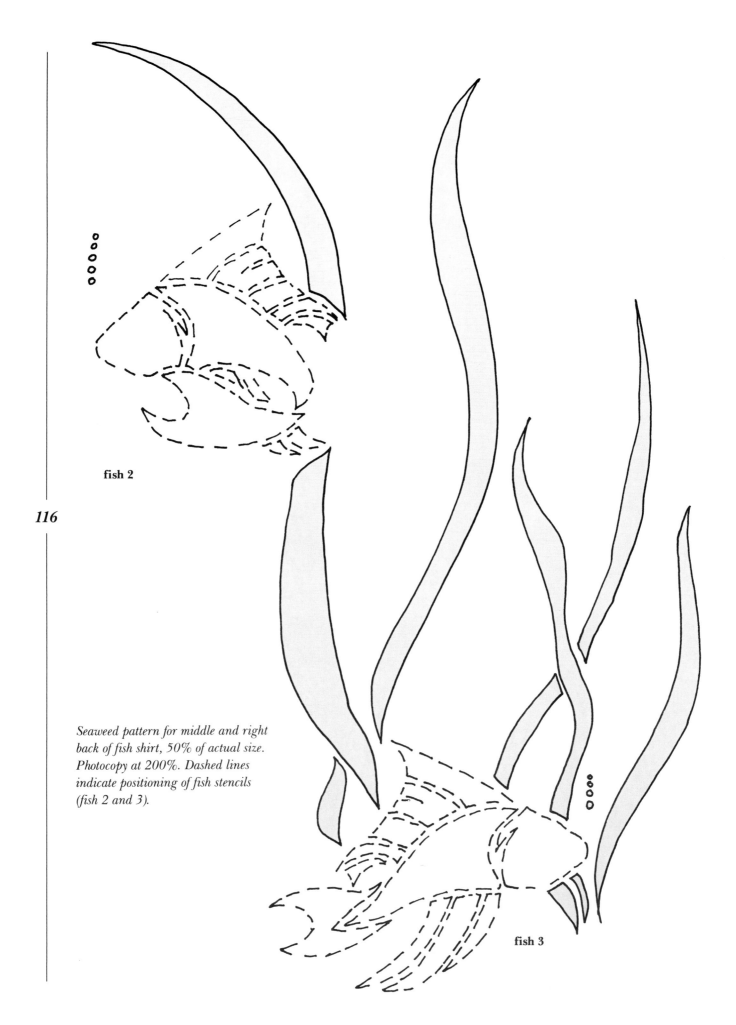

fish 2

116

Seaweed pattern for middle and right
back of fish shirt, 50% of actual size.
Photocopy at 200%. Dashed lines
indicate positioning of fish stencils
(fish 2 and 3).

fish 3

fish 1

Seaweed pattern for front and back of fish shirt, 50% of actual size. Photocopy at 200%. Dashed lines indicate positioning of fish stencil (fish 1).

Wedding Dress

When painting something as important as a wedding dress, do a preliminary test: paint a spare piece of fabric and heat-set it, then take it to the dry cleaners to check how the paint will react to the cleaning process you intend using on the fabric. It would be awful to put a lot of time and effort into producing a magnificent garment to have it all disappear the first time the dress is cleaned.

This is not meant to be an overwhelming design, but a subtle enhancement to the beautiful texture of the fabric. You can also reflect the design by stencilling the same motif in aqua onto an ivory silk for the bridesmaids' and flower girls' dresses. Complete the picture by giving the bride a beautiful bouquet of fresh magnolias!

YOU WILL NEED

❖ Wedding dress or evening dress

❖ Magnolia stencils (page 119)

❖ Basic supplies (see page 10)

❖ Small pearl beads for decorating the dress

❖ Paint: Pale aqua or another color that is close to the color of the fabric

❖ 1 roller

1. Enlarge your stencils and cut them out of drafting film.

2. If you are making up the dress, paint the fabric before sewing up the dress. A raw dupion aqua-colored silk was used on the model dress. Mix the paint to match the color of the fabric exactly.

3. Spray adhesive onto the back of the stencil, being wary not to use too much as it will mark the fabric if it is too wet. Remember, it is only there to hold the stencil in place and to keep the details of the stencil from moving around.

4. Position the bodice motif centrally on the bodice, allowing for seams.

5. Paint the stencil, being very careful not to use too much paint.

6. Stencil the train of the dress, painting the center design and one trailing pattern on one side, then reversing the trailing stencil design to paint the other side.

7. Heat-set the paint using a piece of cotton fabric as a pressing cloth to protect the silk or other delicate fabric from the very hot iron. Consult the Fabric section of the book under the specific fabric for details.

8. If you wish, use pearls around the top of the dress, as in the model. Complete the stencilled designs by highlighting them with drop pearls to match the pearl border at the top.

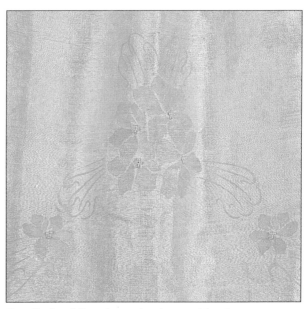

Detail of wedding dress, showing seed beads.

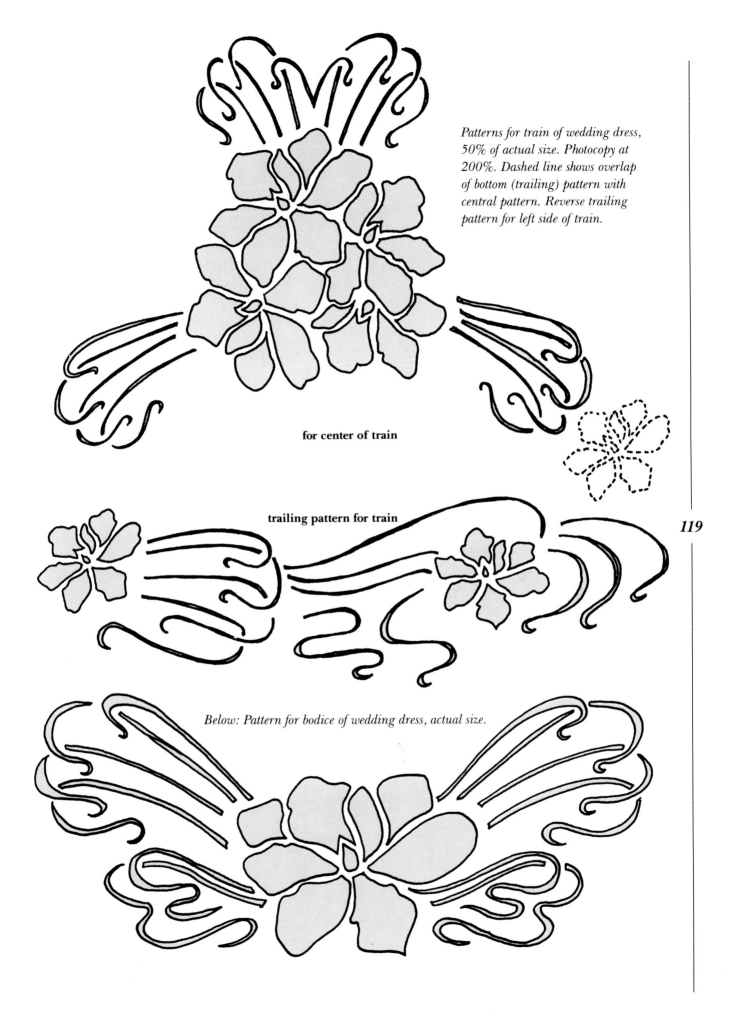

Patterns for train of wedding dress, 50% of actual size. Photocopy at 200%. Dashed line shows overlap of bottom (trailing) pattern with central pattern. Reverse trailing pattern for left side of train.

for center of train

trailing pattern for train

Below: Pattern for bodice of wedding dress, actual size.

119

Cloth Floor Mat

YOU WILL NEED

❖ Heavy calico or light canvas, enough to create the size mat you want

❖ Stencil of your choice

❖ Basic supplies (see page 10)

❖ Fabric paints or acrylic paints

❖ Acrylic house paint for the background

❖ Clear polyurethane varnish

❖ Rollers—one per color

1. Hem your mat with a wide hem, at least 2 inches (5 cm).

2. Paint the mat, back and front, with an acrylic house paint in a neutral color. You may need two coats to cover the canvas. You will find that, as it is a water-based paint, it will cause some shrinkage to the fabric.

3. Stencil the mat with an all-over pattern or a simple scattered pattern of your choice.

4. When the paint is completely dry, coat it back and front with at least three coats of polyurethane varnish, allowing each coat to dry before applying the next one. This will protect the pattern and keep the canvas clean.

Note: For storage, roll the mat, rather than folding it, as the paint will crack. To clean this mat, all you need to do is scrub it—the paint is very resilient. If, after a couple of years, it looks a bit tired, you can give it another coat of polyurethane, or throw it away and start again.

120

Ideas Shop

Wow! Where to start! There are so many ways to use stencilling on fabric—an infinite number of ways you can utilize the skills you have learned so far. Every time you think of one idea, another jumps to mind.

This section is designed to add to the list of things you can already do; the instructions will add to your knowledge without going into the detail of how to do it. Any special considerations are described; this way we can look at more ideas in less space.

When trying out new ideas, always practice on paper first. Invest in a roll of newsprint or butcher's paper and play with designs and ideas. It can be tempting to leap in both feet when trying something new, but spend some time planning; it is worth the effort. This will give you time to assess the colors you want to use, paint swatches of colors and draw and re-draw your design before committing it to the knife.

It is very tempting, once you have cut out your stencil to make do, even if it is not quite right, because of the effort required to recut it. You are better off cutting your losses (pardon the pun) and *recutting your stencil*. If you are not absolutely happy with the design, it will drive you mad, or you will never wear it/use it and it will end up being a waste of effort. Persevere and get it right before you stencil your garment or project. You will congratulate yourself on your patience when you are constantly rewarded by a job well done and the accolades that go with it.

Getting it right can also be profitable. A garment that catches the eye of others has the potential to create a market for your work. Stencilling on fabric is far easier, just as effective, and ultimately will make more money than hand painting or screen printing garments. Designs can be readily reproduced by stencilling, but each one is an individual work of art; that has to be worth more! Your personal signature on the corner of the scarf or on the T-shirt adds that touch of class.

There is usually a way to achieve what you want. It may not be easy; it may mean a lot of trial and error, a lot of research, and a lot of playing around with designs and different paints. *Don't ever be told you can't do it!* Many people enjoy spending their time telling you what you can't do. Take pleasure in proving them wrong. There are not too many things that are impossible when it comes to stencilling on fabric. Some of the different things you can do are given below.

Teapot Design Place Mats

The fabric with the black background was the source of inspiration for this stencil.

I used store-bought white place mats. The design was inspired by the fabric shown in the photograph. (Fabrics can be a great source of inspiration for designs.) The teapot and teacup designs would look great in a wall hanging. The borders of the wall hanging could be made of a fabric that uses one of the colors in the stencil, or a tint or shade of it or its complement (see the color section for more about color).

Paint the mats with a couple of coats of clear polyurethane varnish after you have stencilled the designs onto them to protect them from the rigors of the dinner table. If you can't find ready-made mats, make them yourself out of heavy-duty canvas.

Teapot design for place mats, 66% of actual size. Photocopy at 150%.

Teacup design for place mats, 66% of actual size.
Photocopy at 150%.

123

Redback Spider and Web for Old Jeans

Redback spiders add an appropriate final touch to "slashed" or "grunge-look" jeans. The denim is nice and soft and takes the paint beautifully, because it is so old. Rather than cut a separate stencil to paint on the spider's red back, I painted the red part on freehand with a small paintbrush. Of course, new jeans also can be stencilled, and dressed up with some studs, beads, or embroidery.

124

Spider and web pattern, actual size.

Rose Tablecloth

The rose design was inspired by the damask design embossed in the fabric. If you're making up your own design from a fabric, trace the design onto tracing paper, tidy the image up so that the lines will work in a stencil, plan the stencil bridges, and then transfer the design onto stencil film. On the tablecloth, the rose has been turned into a swag with a bow. The single rose adds the finishing touch to the table napkins.

Place a bow in the corners of the cloth and in the center of each of the long sides; position the swag along the sides. By reversing the swag stencil in the center of the cloth you can create a garland. See the section on Positioning Stencils for more details about stencil placement.

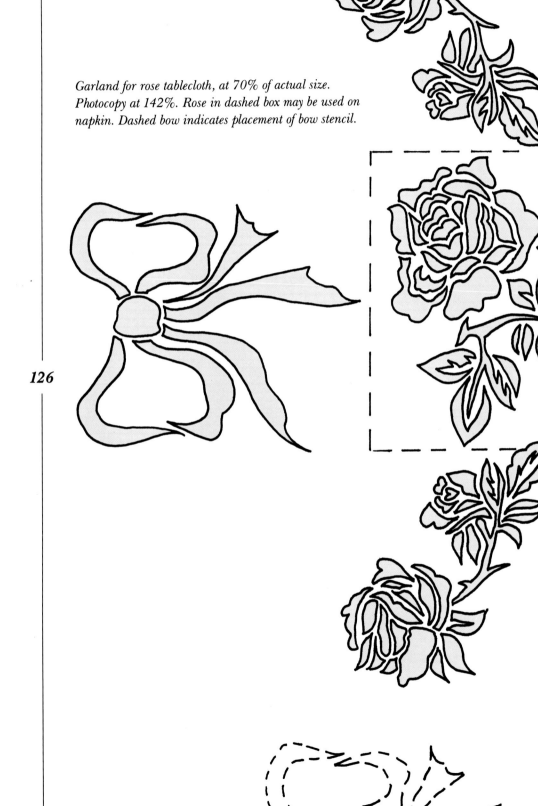

Garland for rose tablecloth, at 70% of actual size. Photocopy at 142%. Rose in dashed box may be used on napkin. Dashed bow indicates placement of bow stencil.

126

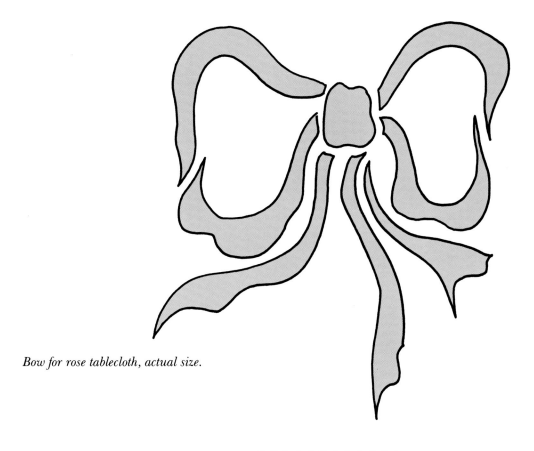

Bow for rose tablecloth, actual size.

❖❖❖❖❖❖❖❖❖❖❖

Christmas Tablecloth and Napkins

One way to brighten up your Christmas table is to stencil a wreath onto your tablecloth, and make napkins to match. They look great in red or green.

Garland for Christmas tablecloth, 50% of actual size. Photocopy at 200%.

Bow for Christmas napkin, actual size.

Horn for Christmas tablecloth, actual size.

Framed Print

Stencil a bunch of flowers onto a piece of silk or calico, then stitch it onto a backing cardboard and have it framed, or frame it yourself. It makes a nice change from prints and is an inexpensive alternative to original paintings. Be sure to leave several inches of fabric around your design so that you can turn the edges to the back of the cardboard and sew them in place with embroidery thread or other strong thread before framing.

The different shadings on the stencil design mean you need to cut out three separate stencils to create the design, as indicated on the key. Each of the three stencils is used in turn to make the design. *The shadings do not indicate different colors of paint; they indicate from which stencil the parts should be cut.* You can see from the painted design that the different parts of the design run into one another. If you tried to cut them all from one stencil, the details would be lost, because there is almost no room for bridges in the design to hold it all together.

To make the stencils: On the first stencil, block in all the parts of the design that were hatched on the original pattern (1 in the key). On the second stencil, block in all the parts that were a solid color (2 in the key). On the third stencil, block in all the areas that were stippled (3 in the key). Cut out the areas of each stencil that you have blocked in.

To paint: Position stencil 1 on the fabric and paint each part of the design on that stencil in whatever colors you like: Paint all the stems, flowers, etc. on that stencil. Remove the first stencil, let the paint dry, and carefully position stencil 2 over it, using the previously painted design as a placement guide. (You can also use registration marks if you like to align the stencils.) After you finish stencil 2, position and paint stencil 3. The placing of the second and third stencils is critical because the different parts of the design butt up to the edge of the other parts of the design. There is no space between them. The stencilled design should end up looking like a painting of a bunch of flowers, rather than a stencil. Practice using a single flower until you get the idea.

130

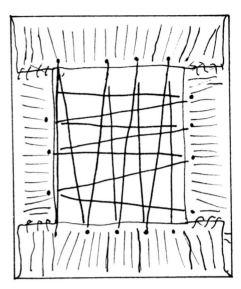

Borders of print are stretched around a cardboard and stitched in place on the cardboard back with embroidery thread or other strong thread.

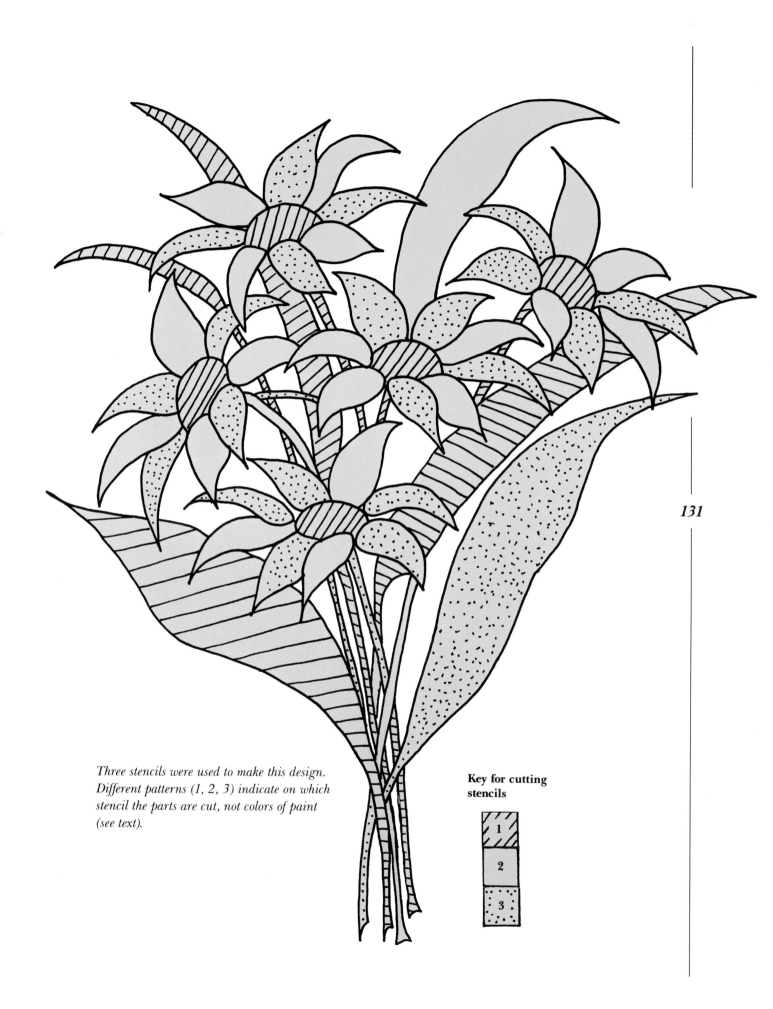

Three stencils were used to make this design. Different patterns (1, 2, 3) indicate on which stencil the parts are cut, not colors of paint (see text).

Key for cutting stencils

1
2
3

131

Muffin Tablecloth

There are endless ideas for tablecloths, which make them great gifts or items for the church bazaar. Muffins stencilled onto the cloth, or cupcakes or ice cream cones for children's parties are just a couple of ideas.

Muffin and border patterns for tablecloth, at 80%. Photocopy at 125%. Dashed line indicates position of pattern overlap for repeats.

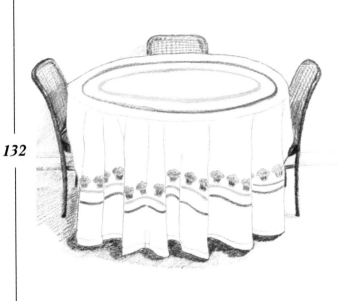

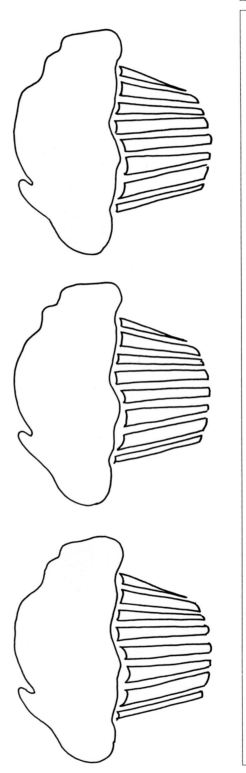

Scarves

Scarves offer huge opportunities to let your creative juices flow! Buy a few yards (metres) of silk, cut it into long rectangular or square scarves, and explore the possibilities. You can see some of them in the photo.

There are many ways of painting on silk. Normally, paints made especially for silk are contained or restricted by using gutta, a medium that stops the paints from spreading all over the silk uncontrollably by creating little walls. The gutta, which comes in a colorless as well as colored forms, may be removed or may become a permanent part of the design. Unless you use the stencil as a guide to apply the gutta

and then paint within those confines with silk paints, silk paints can really only be used as a background for stencilling, because if you try to stencil directly without gutta, the silk paints will spread out in all directions and blur all the contours of the design.

This spreading of the silk paint can be used to advantage, however, in freehand painting on silk, which will give you a special look. Paint the piece of silk overall with silk paint. When the silk paint dries, stencil a design on the silk using a fabric paint. This method was used when making the blue scarf shown in the photo. Be careful not to put too much fabric paint on the silk when you stencil, because too much paint will become hard and crisp, which defeats the purpose of using silk.

Geometric designs, borders and lines can be created using removable cellophane tape. Simply lay out the scarf, hold it firmly in place with tape, and mark out the borders and stripes using tape.

A contrast can be created by painting a pastel stripe on a dark background, or a neutral look with cream color on white silk with a matching fringe to finish it off. The poppy scarf shown in the photo was made to match the poppy dress shown in the fashion section.

Scarves can be finished with a narrow hem that is machine-stitched, or the edges may be hand rolled to give a really professional look. This is not difficult to achieve, but it does take a little more time than machine stitching. To roll a hem, use a fine thread the same color as the edge fabric of the scarf and a long thin needle. Roll the edge of the fabric around the needle and stitch it in place on the back of the scarf with blind hemming stitches.

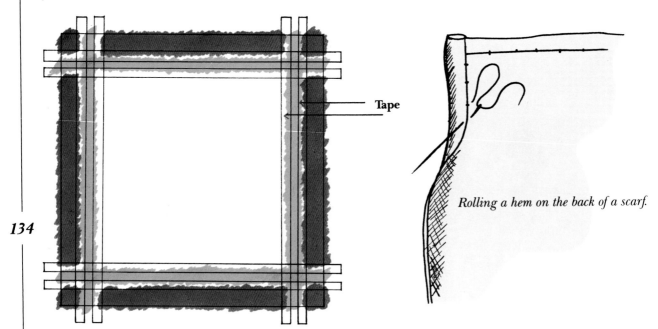

Tape

Rolling a hem on the back of a scarf.

Stencilling borders on a square scarf, using masking tape as a guide.

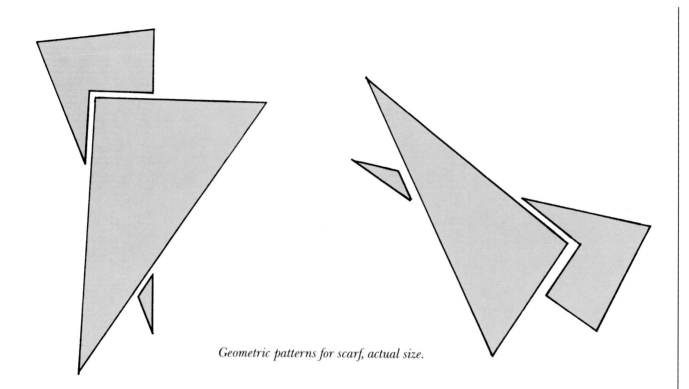

Geometric patterns for scarf, actual size.

Leaf patterns for scarf, actual size.

Birds pattern for scarf, actual size.

Fish pattern for scarf, actual size.

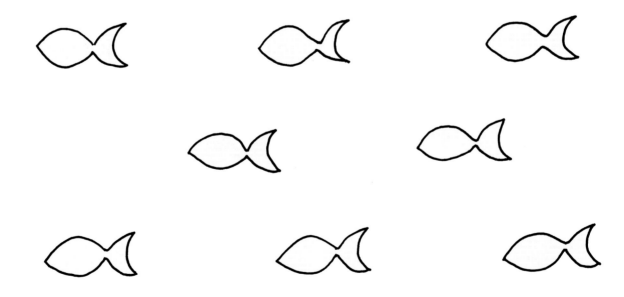

Border patterns for scarf, at 88%. Photocopy at 113%. Dashed line indicates position of repeat.

137

Cow Dish Towel

Dish towels are a wonderful way of promoting something: an occasion like Christmas or Halloween, or for raising money at a bazaar or fair. Purchase plain linen dish towels and stencil them with all kinds of things; they sell really well and are very quick and easy to make.

Pattern for cow dish towel, 70% of actual size. Photocopy at 142%.

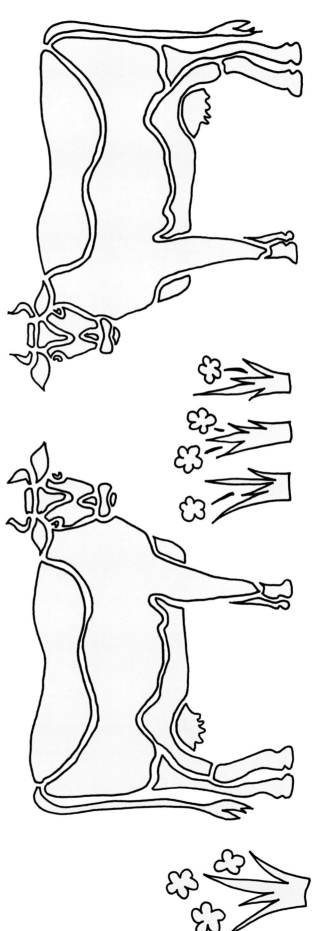

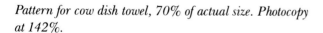

Stencilled Team T-Shirts

This is a handy way to number team shirts. The numeral had to be painted in white first on our example to mask the stripes in the fabric below; then it was repainted in yellow. You can make the numerals as large or small as they need to be.

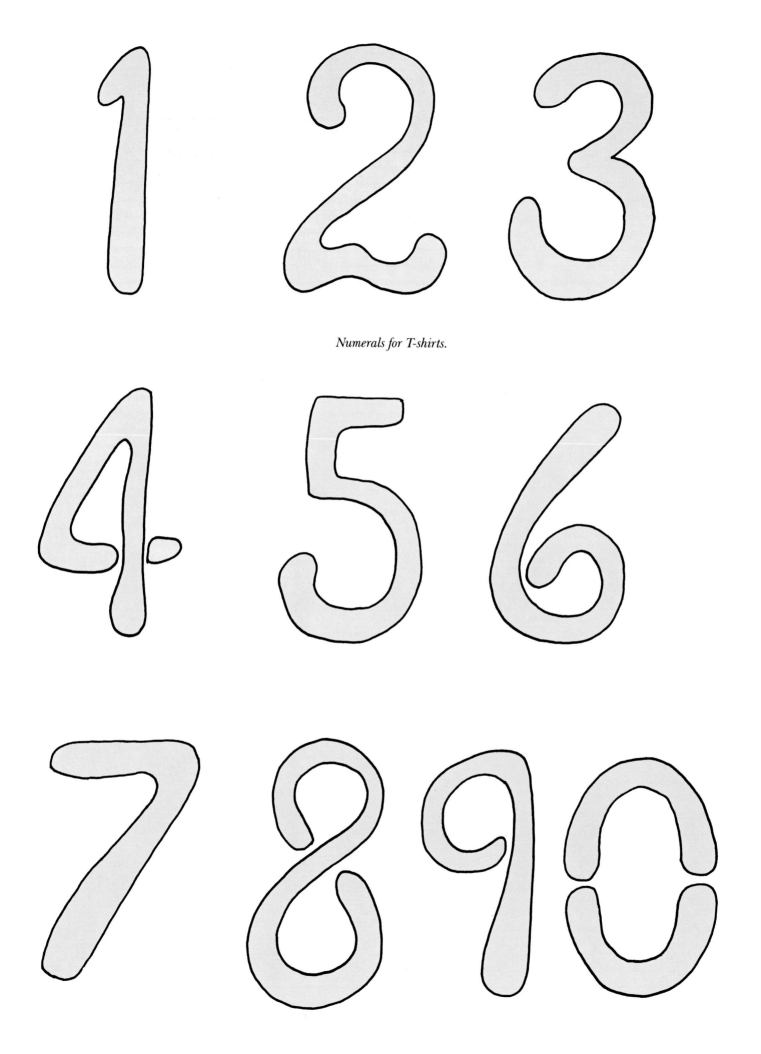

Numerals for T-shirts.

Bags

You can stencil just about anything onto a bag—a gift bag, ballet bag, stuff bag, shopping tote—and make it a special bag. A Christmas-tree or holly-stencilled calico bag makes a nice alternative to gift wrapping at Christmas time.

Gardening Gloves

Gardening gloves and a gardening mat stencilled with matching designs make good items for a bazaar or fair; package them up with a potted plant and you will have something different to sell.

Gum Blossom Shirt

The gum tree blossom pattern can be used
instead of fish to decorate a shirt.

Gum tree blossom pattern at 50%.
Photocopy at 200%.

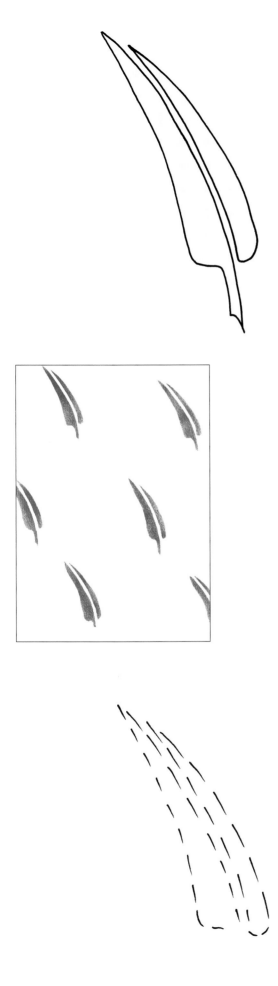

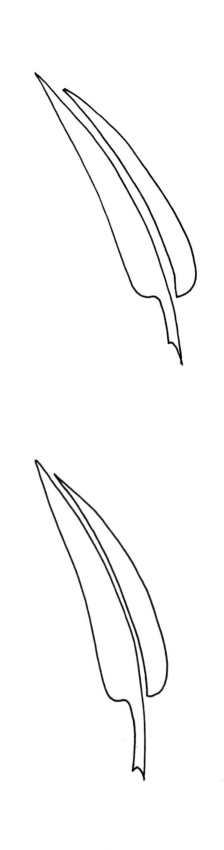

Pattern for the back of the Bird-of-Paradise wall hanging at 95%. Photocopy at 105%. Dashed line shows positioning of repeat. Inset shows stencilled backing fabric.

Index

144